ON CRIMES AND
PUNISHMENTS

The Library of Liberal Arts

OSKAR PIEST, FOUNDER

ON CRIMES AND PUNISHMENTS

CESARE BECCARIA

Translated, with an introduction, by
HENRY PAOLUCCI

The Library of Liberal Arts
published by

Macmillan Publishing Company
New York
Collier Macmillan Publishers
London

Cesare Beccaria: 1738-1794

ON CRIMES AND PUNISHMENTS was originally published
in 1764

• • • • • • • • • • • • • • • • • • • •

Macmillan Publishing Company
866 Third Avenue
New York, New York, 10022
Collier Macmillan Canada, Inc.

PRINTING   17 18 19 20 21   YEAR   1 2 3 4 5

Library of Congress Catalog Card Number: 61-18589
ISBN 0-02-391360-6

CONTENTS
· · · · · · · · · · · · · · · ·

ON CRIMES AND PUNISHMENTS

INTRODUCTION

If at one time it seemed likely that the historical spirit
(the spirit which strove to understand the classical jurisprudence of Rome and the Twelve Tables, and the Lex
Salica, and law of all ages and climes) was fatalistic and
enimical to reform, that time already lies in the past. . . .
Now-a-days we may see the office of historical research as
that of explaining, and therefore lightening, the pressure
that the past must exercise upon the present, and the present upon the future. To-day we study the day before
yesterday, in order that yesterday may not paralyze to-day,
and to-day may not paralyze to-morrow.[1]

Frederic W. Maitland

I. REPUTATION

Historians of criminal law agree, almost without exception,
that the "glory of having expelled the use of torture from every
tribunal throughout Christendom" belongs primarily to Cesare
Beccaria.[2] His treatise *On Crimes and Punishments* (*Dei Delitti
e delle Pene*), newly translated here, is generally acknowledged
to have had "more practical effect than any other treatise ever
written in the long campaign against barbarism in criminal
law and procedure." [3]

The work was originally published anonymously in Tuscany

[1] Frederic William Maitland, *The Collected Papers of Frederic William
Maitland* (Cambridge, 1911), III, 438-39.

[2] See Leon Radzinowicz, *A History of English Criminal Law* (New York,
1948), I, 277-83; James Anson Farrer, *Crimes and Punishments, Including
a New Translation of Beccaria's "Dei Delitti e delle Pene"* (London, 1880),
pp. 3, 46; Coleman Phillipson, *Three Criminal Law Reformers* (London,
1923), pp. 32-34, 100-02.

[3] Harry Elmer Barnes and Howard Becker, *Social Thought from Lore
to Science* (Washington, 1952), I, 551-52.

in 1764. Almost at once, as if an exposed nerve had been touched, all Europe was stirred to excitement. The first English translator, writing eighteen months after its original appearance, noted that the work had already passed through six editions in Italian, that several French editions had appeared, and that "perhaps no book, on any subject, was ever received with more avidity, more generally read, or more universally applauded." [4]

The French translation of 1766, by the Abbé Morellet, had been the vehicle for rapid diffusion of the work through all the enlightened salons, coffee houses, and courts of Europe. In Paris, d'Alembert, Helvetius, Buffon, d'Holbach, and the visiting Hume praised it enthusiastically. Voltaire, who later graced it with an elaborate commentary, hailed it as "le code de l'humanité." [5] Frederick II of Prussia expressed his admiration by complaining, in a letter to Voltaire, that Beccaria "has left hardly anything to be gleaned after him" in the sphere of criminal law.[6] Maria Teresa of Austria and the Grand Duke Leopold of Tuscany publicly declared their intention to be guided by the book's principles in the reformation of their laws, while Catherine the Great of Russia called upon its author to reside at her court and attend to the necessary reforms in person.[7]

In England, it was Beccaria's treatise, as Sir William Holdsworth states, that "helped Blackstone to crystallize his ideas." [8] Upon reading it Jeremy Bentham was moved to write: "Oh, my master, first evangelist of Reason . . . you who have made so many useful excursions into the path of utility, what is

[4] Cesare Beccaria, *An Essay on Crimes and Punishments*, tr. unknown (London, 1767), Preface of the Translator, pp. iii-iv.

[5] See Cesare Beccaria, *Des délits et des peines*, tr. J. A. S. Collin de Plancy (2nd edn.; Paris, 1823), p. xviii.

[6] Voltaire, Francois-Marie Arouet, *Oeuvres complètes*, ed. L. Moland (Paris, 1877-85), L, 265.

[7] On Beccaria's influence, see Phillipson, *Three Criminal Law Reformers*, pp. 83-106.

[8] Cited by Radzinowicz, *History of English Criminal Law*, I, 346.

there left for us to do?—Never to turn aside from that path." [9]
Across the Atlantic, John Adams took inspiration from the
book for his defense of the British soldiers involved in the
Boston Massacre of 1770; and long after the trial, many of
those who had been present recalled vividly, as John Quincy
Adams later reported, "the electrical effect produced upon the
jury and upon the immense and excited auditory, by the first
sentence with which he opened his defense, which was [a]
citation from the then recently published work of Beccaria." [10]
In the midst of such widespread approbation, the slight ad-
verse criticism the work initially attracted proved to be of
little consequence. The Church of Rome had placed the treatise on the Index in 1766, condemning it for its extremely rationalistic presuppositions.[11] But in Beccaria's own Milan the
representative of Austrian despotic rule, Count Firmian, personally defended the author against charges of sacrilege and
political subversion, and the Austrian government itself was
moved to honor him by assigning him a professorial chair in
the Palatine schools of Milan.[12] By that time, however, critics
frustrated in their attacks on Beccaria's work were already re-
directing their efforts to the less formidable task of impugning
his character.

II. CHARACTER OF THE AUTHOR

Cesare Beccaria was born on March 15, 1738, of an aristocratic Milanese family that had long ceased to exercise political
functions commensurate with its title. After eight years of
what he later called "fanatical education" [13] under the Jesuits

9 MSS. University College, London, No. 32. Cited in Élie Halévy, *The
Growth of Philosophical Radicalism* (London, 1928), p. 21.
10 John Adams, *The Works of John Adams* (Boston, 1856), II, 238-39n.
11 See article on Beccaria in *Enciclopedia Cattolica* (Vatican City, 1949),
Vol. II, col. 1126.
12 See Phillipson, *Three Criminal Law Reformers*, pp. 14, 21.
13 See Marcello T. Maestro, *Voltaire and Beccaria as Reformers of
Criminal Law* (New York, 1942), p. 52.

of Parma, he studied, without distinguishing himself, at the University of Pavia, where he received a degree in 1758. In 1761, encouraged by his friends Pietro and Alessandro Verri, he boldly contracted a marriage which his father had sought by every possible means to prevent. But the experience of attempting to earn a living, and the specter of poverty, soon unsettled his resolve. In a melodramatic scene staged by his resourceful friends, he and his frightened bride humbly begged and obtained parental forgiveness and support. Young Beccaria's resentment against the authority of the aristocratic paterfamilias—an authority which he would inherit upon his father's death—was later movingly expressed in several passages of his celebrated treatise.

The Verri brothers also encouraged Beccaria in his intellectual exploits. For the elder brother, Pietro, ten years his senior, young Cesare came to feel, he later said, "the same enthusiasm of friendship that Montaigne felt for Étienne de la Boétie." [14] He was everything Cesare dreamed of being. After a rebellious youth of wild love affairs and heated family quarrels, Pietro had successfully launched himself on a literary career, only to interrupt it suddenly by enlisting in the Austrian army. He attained the rank of captain and distinguished himself for bravery in the campaigns of the Seven Years' War against Prussia. When he returned to Milan in 1760, he undertook, with his younger brother Alessandro, to initiate a program of political, social, and literary reforms. With the young Milanese intelligentsia rallying around them, they formed a society later known as the "academy of fists," dedicated to waging relentless war against economic disorder, bureaucratic petty tyranny, religious narrow-mindedness, and intellectual pedantry. To propagate their ideas they eventually established a periodical, Il Caffè, modeled on Joseph Addison's Spectator.

It was as a member of this avant-gardist "academy of fists" that Beccaria first took up his pen in behalf of humanity. The heated discussions that animated the Verri house, where the reformers regularly met, fascinated his attention. Under Pietro

[14] Beccaria, Opere, ed. Sergio Romagnoli (Florence, 1958), II, 867.

Verri's guidance, he began to read the enlightened authors of France and England: Montesquieu, first of all, then Helvetius, who taught him the principle of "utility," then d'Alembert, Diderot, Buffon, Hume—"illustrious names," he later wrote, "which no one can hear without emotion." [15] He was an avid reader and an attentive listener. But, except for occasional outbursts of compassion and irrepressible indignation when the discussion turned on the sad tale of man's inhumanity to man, he said little, and wrote only when his friends assigned a topic, elaborated the subject matter, and literally pieced his fragmentary utterances together for him. His first publication, a treatise "On Remedies for the Monetary Disorders of Milan in the Year 1762," was thus written at the suggestion and with the constant prodding of Pietro Verri, who had expert knowledge of the subject, and who, when the work was attacked soon after publication, personally took up the burden of defending it.

On Crimes and Punishments was composed with similar prodding and assistance. Pietro Verri, Beccaria gratefully acknowledged in a letter to the Abbé Morellet, "gave me the strength to write; and I owe it to him that the manuscript of On Crimes . . ., which he generously transcribed for me in his own hand, did not end up in the flames." [16] When a rumor began to circulate that the work was not really Beccaria's, Pietro took care to define very precisely his role in its composition. "I suggested the topic to him," he conceded, "and most of the ideas came out of daily conversation between Beccaria, Alessandro, Lambertenghi, and myself." But the book itself, he asserted unequivocally, "is by the Marquis Beccaria." Admittedly young Cesare "knew nothing about our criminal system" at the time the topic was suggested, but what he lacked his friends were eager and able to supply. Alessandro Verri had assumed the official post of "protector of prisoners" in Milan, and therefore had firsthand knowledge of penal practices. Pietro had already begun to compile materials for a his-

15 Maestro, *Voltaire and Beccaria*, p. 52.
16 Beccaria, *Opere*, II, 867.

tory of torture, and had a host of details on the tip of his tongue. Beccaria—Pietro's account continues—"began to write down some of his ideas on loose pieces of paper; we urged him on with enthusiasm, stimulating him so much that he soon got together a great quantity of them. After dinner we would take a walk, discuss the errors of criminal jurisprudence, argue, raise questions, and in the evening he would write. But writing is so laborious for him, and costs him so much effort that after an hour he collapses and can't go on. When he had amassed the materials, I wrote them out, arranged them in order, and thus made a book out of them." [17]

Because of Beccaria's fear that he might be prosecuted for it, the book thus shaped by enthusiastic collaboration was originally issued anonymously. But once it was clear that the Milanese political authorities welcomed the treatise, anonymity was discarded. The happiest result of the publication was, of course, the attention it drew from the Parisian intelligentsia. After the French translation appeared, the Abbé Morellet, writing in the name of the Encyclopedists, invited Pietro Verri to visit Paris with Beccaria so that due honor might be accorded the author of *On Crimes and Punishments*. Unfortunately, Pietro could not accept; his recent appointment as head of a commission charged with revising the provincial laws obliged him to remain in Milan. Beccaria, fearful of the impression he would make, in person and alone, at first refused to budge. But Pietro was master. As he had regulated Beccaria's marital affairs, as he had directed his reading and writing, so he assigned him the task of journeying to Paris to receive the honors of the world. On October 2, 1766, accompanied by Alessandro Verri, Beccaria took his departure, following his escort, it is said, not like a hero on his way to a triumph, but like a condemned prisoner on his way to the gallows.

Halfway there, he threatened to turn back. "By God," Pietro Verri wrote to spur him on, "I owe you the candor to tell you a truth in writing that I might not have the heart to tell you face to face, and it is that there is a puerile side to your character that greatly detracts from the esteem to which you are entitled. . . . This European trip is certain to cure you, and it is the only thing that can cure you." [18]

In Paris, Beccaria was indeed received with adoration. The most famous personalities of the day escorted him from salon to salon, where he was honored as a great benefactor of humanity. But he made a very bad impression. Morellet thus represents the fiasco in his *Mémoires:*

> . . . he arrived somber and anxious, and one could hardly get a word out of him. His friend, on the contrary, a personable fellow, gay, and of ready wit, soon attracted to himself the solicitudes and attentions of society. It was this, finally, that completely turned poor Beccaria's head. After having spent but three weeks or a month in Paris, he went home alone, leaving us, as a pledge, the count Verri. Toward the end of his sojourn he was so irritated mentally and emotionally that he would close himself up in his room at the hotel where . . . I often went to keep him company, trying, without success, to calm him.[19]

Before it took place, Pietro Verri exerted every possible pressure to prevent Beccaria's homeward flight. "You must not forget," he wrote, "that, having attracted to yourself the regard of mankind . . . , you cannot hope that the act of timidity you contemplate will remain hidden." He warned Beccaria that some people would say he was an effeminate, childish imbecile, without backbone, "incapable of living away from his mother." Others would think he fled because Paris had slighted him, and "all sorts of things are bound to be said about your character which I can darkly foresee and which you can imagine as well as I, if you reflect on it." [20]

But for once Beccaria asserted his independence. Instinctively he realized that he was not able, as a man, to live up to the reputation of the book. Hoping to salvage that reputation, and eventually his own as author, he chose to disappoint the

18 Beccaria, *Opere*, I, xxxiii.
19 Abbé Morellet, *Mémoires* (Paris, 1823), I, 167-68.
20 Beccaria, *Opere*, I, xxxi.

expectations of the "academy of fists" and to alienate his dearest friend by taking flight.

Once home, Beccaria never ventured forth again. In Milan, where he could not conceal the truth about himself, there was much ridicule and gossip. And yet, he was the gainer. Enjoying the patronage of the Austrian government, he lapsed into an Epicurean indolence. From 1768 until his death in 1794 he occupied a series of public offices that were all more or less sinecures; but isolated as he was from his old friend he was not able, in all that time, to produce a single writing worthy of public attention.

Abroad, however, especially in France and England, a legend began to shape itself about his name. Admirers of his book, ignorant of the political situation in Milan, interpreted Beccaria's long silence romantically, as evidence of cruel suppression at the hands of a tyrannical and bigoted government. "Athens," an English admirer wrote, "would have honored him; Rome would have given him a triumph; in Italy he is silent." A French translator concluded: "If he who at twenty-six could write the immortal On Crimes and Punishments had lived in a land of freedom, we would have had other masterpieces, and posterity would not have to regard with astonishment the silence in which Beccaria kept himself for the rest of his life." [21]

While Beccaria lived, such a legend could not have gained credence in Italy. But after his death, Pietro Verri, who survived him by three years, prepared a way for its eventual cultivation. With the man himself no longer present to embarrass the cause, "Citizen Verri," on December 13, 1797, called upon the municipality of Milan to erect "a monument of recognition to the immortal Beccaria." [22] Thus the man who might have been the most devastating witness against him undertook to silence public criticism—and very nearly succeeded. Except for the scruple of scholars, Beccaria would be remembered today,

[21] Beccaria, *Des délits et des peines* (Paris, 1823), p. xxvi.
[22] See Piero Calamandrei's introduction to Cesare Beccaria, *Dei Delitti e delle Pene* (Florence, 1950), p. 61.

everywhere in the world, not only as a literary champion of the cause of humanity but also as one of its heroic, long-suffering martyrs.

III. STYLE AND CONTENT

Much has been written about the style of the work. In the late eighteenth century, a number of neo-classical purists denied that it had a style in the strict sense. For instance, Giuseppe Baretti, the distinguished literary critic and friend of Samuel Johnson, did not hesitate to describe it as a "wretched little thing bastardly written." [23] Some critics who knew the complex story of its composition—how a mass of ideas from the French rationalists had been hastily scribbled by Beccaria, transcribed and reordered by Verri, drastically revised by subsequent editors and translators, especially by Morellet, whose paragraphing and reordered sequence Beccaria willingly adopted as an improvement over the original—argued that *On Crimes and Punishments* ought not to be considered as the work of an individual author with a distinctive personality and style of his own. And yet even a cursory reading of its pages suffices to discredit such an allegation. His friends no doubt supplied the ideas and what little logical sequence is to be found in it, but, as Pietro Verri remarked, "the poetry of the work is Beccaria's very own." [24]

That there is poetry in the treatise critics of the romantic era readily acknowledged. Ugo Foscolo, rejecting the neo-classical standards, characterized its style as "absolute and secure," [25] and subsequent scholars have remarked that while the writing is uneven in parts the effect of the whole borders on the sublime. Many of its sentences, especially those in which the author offers to display his mastery of "geometric" reasoning, are hopelessly involuted. Clauses are strung together in a maze of complexity, as if the author were attempting to express involved thought with maximum precision, when in fact

---

23 *Ibid.*, p. 46.   24 *Ibid.*, p. 61.   25 *Ibid.*, p. 49.

he is merely trying to veil his juridical and historical ignorance, which was notorious. Sympathetic translators often presume to break up such sentences, hoping thereby to resolve the riddle of their meaning. But the result is invariably disastrous. Syntactical simplification merely lays bare the emptiness of arguments that Beccaria's involuted language manages to conceal. Stylistically, moreover, the labored passages serve admirably to throw the truly eloquent sequences into high relief. In Chapter XIV, for instance, after a painfully long and complicated discussion of the utility of offering impunity to criminals who agree to give evidence against their companions, Beccaria suddenly interrupts himself to exclaim: ". . . but I torment myself uselessly trying to overcome the remorse I feel in authorizing the inviolable laws, the monument of public trust, the basis of human morality, to countenance treachery and dissimulation."

The style is, in other words, that of an impassioned plea—a style suitable for a work pertaining to the practical and productive spheres of juridical discourse rather than to the theoretic. As employed by Beccaria, its object is not to demonstrate what the law *is*, but rather to incite men to *make* it what the author thinks it *ought to be*. Bentham has carefully drawn the distinction, contrasting two basic kinds of juridical writing— the expository, concerned with ascertaining what the law is, and the censorial, treating of what it ought to be. Beccaria, he has asserted emphatically, "may be styled the father of *Censorial Jurisprudence*." Montesquieu had indicated the direction, but his own *Spirit of the Laws* was, according to Bentham, "a work of mixed kind," part expository, part censorial. Before Montesquieu, of course, "all was unmixed barbarism." [26]

In his introductory statement "To the Reader," Beccaria warns those who would criticize him that he means to proceed in the "geometric spirit," establishing what ought to be in the sphere of law by systematic deduction from a set of self-evident principles which his reader must be intelligent enough not to expect him to prove. He is aware that his principles cannot be

[26] Jeremy Bentham, *A Fragment on Government*, ed. F. C. Montague (London, 1891), p. 105, n. 2.

"induced" by studying things as they are, especially not in the sphere of criminal procedures, where gross error, ignorance, and malice have reigned for centuries. But that is their virtue, not their vice.

According to Beccaria, the fundamental principle that ought to govern the entire sphere of legislation is self-evidently that of "the greatest happiness to be shared by the greatest number." This principle has never actually determined the laws of men, but enlightened thinkers, he says, have always acknowledged its primacy and have already made use of it to discover the various subordinate principles that ought to regulate industry, commerce, foreign affairs, and the relations between sovereigns and their subjects. One area not yet effectively explored in the light of that principle is that of crimes and punishments. "Few persons," Beccaria writes, not in the least attempting to conceal his practical intent, "have studied and fought against the cruelty of punishments and the irregularities of criminal procedures, a part of legislation that is as fundamental as it is widely neglected in almost all of Europe." To study and to fight against the present situation amount to the same, in Beccaria's judgment, for he believes that the situation is sustained entirely by ignorance. To focus light upon it is to destroy it.

In the first chapter Beccaria raises the basic questions he means to explore:

But what are to be the proper punishments for such crimes? Is the death-penalty really *useful* and *necessary* for the security and good order of society? Are torture and torments *just*, and do they attain the *end* for which laws are instituted? What is the best way to prevent crimes? Are the same punishments equally effective for all times? What influence have they on customary behavior?

These problems, he urges, must be analyzed with "geometric precision." To discover the principles that ought to govern such an analysis Beccaria directs his readers to "consult the human heart," where nature itself has imprinted them.

Political community, Beccaria's heart tells him, is, or rather, ought to be the result of an accord entered into by men in order to guarantee for themselves the maximum enjoyment of personal liberty. Each individual willingly sacrifices to the political community only so much of his liberty as "suffices to induce others to defend it." Laws are, or ought to be, simply the necessary conditions of this "social contract," and punishments under the law ought to have no other purpose than to defend the sum of sacrificed shares of liberty "against private usurpations by individuals." Punishments aiming at any other end are "useless" and by their very nature unjust.

These rationalistic ideas of majoritarian hedonism, social contract, and utility were commonplace enough in Beccaria's time. The novelty of his book consists in his censorial application of them. His presentation proceeds as a kind of trial. From the beginning it is clear that, in the author's judgment, a terrible crime has been committed against humanity. The principles that ought to govern all human relations have been and are still being violated in a most barbarous manner. Under accusation before the court of world opinion are almost all the rulers, legislators, jurists, magistrates, policemen, and jailers of the past and present. It is useless to argue against the impassioned author that he misrepresents many of the juridical theories and practices brought under accusation. It is of no concern to him that the principles he professes are inadequate to embrace in any meaningful way the facts of Western legal experience; that no nation, past or present, was ever formed by a social contract; that law is not and never has been merely a bond of equals, as the social contract theory assumes. Neither is it of concern to him that, in the attempt to realize the greatest happiness of the greatest number, utility itself may dictate the necessity of torture, severity of punishments, and even the death penalty. What is of concern to him he has plainly stated in words that limit precisely the use to which the doctrine of his book can properly be applied. Recognizing the censorial force of the words, John Adams made use of them, before a hostile court, to open his defense of the British soldiers implicated in the Boston Massacre:

. . . if, by defending the rights of man and of unconquerable truth, I should help to save from the spasm and agonies of death some wretched victim of tyranny or of no less fatal ignorance, the thanks and tears of one innocent mortal in his transports of joy would console me for the contempt of all mankind.[27]

IV. HISTORICAL SIGNIFICANCE

Beccaria's *On Crimes and Punishments* played a significant role, historically, in the final phase of the long struggle between the hereditary aristocrats of Europe and the great monarchic families bent on destroying the independent authority of the so-called intermediate powers. Basing their rule on the ever increasing wealth and numbers of the rising bourgeoisie, the great monarchs gradually succeeded in depriving the aristocratic class of its political and military functions, if not of its leisure. No longer able to justify their privileged status by their willingness and ability to fight, ambitious noblemen took to the pen. Some labored, by means of words, to validate old feudal claims, recognition of which their ancestors had extorted by violence. Others, resigning themselves to a courtier's life, attempted to justify on historical or rational grounds the prerogatives of absolute monarchs. Still others courted the rising bourgeoisie, hoping to establish themselves as a new aristocracy of intellect and sensibility by defending the "rights of men and inviolable truth" against all the oppressive forces of darkness.

Beccaria's treatise was a contribution to the third of these aristocratic causes. In the interests of mankind, its author appealed to the enlightened rulers of Europe to use all their coercive power to crush the petty tyrannies of aristocratic privilege and bureaucratic abuse. In its immediate sense, the appeal seemed, indeed, to serve the cause of monarchs against the intermediary powers. But its ultimate effect was to precipitate the ruin of both. Throughout Europe the revolutions that

[27] See John Adams, *Works*, II, 238. The source in Beccaria's treatise is Chapter I, Introduction (p. 10).

swept away aristocratic privilege did not cease until they had
swept away monarchic pretensions as well. And they proved
to be viciously brutal revolutions, in some instances, precisely
because enlightened monarchs had encouraged the propagation
of works that exaggerated the evils as well as the powers of the
ancien régime.

To what extent Beccaria's work exaggerated the evils of
criminal procedure in his day his own grandson, Alessandro
Manzoni—Italy's greatest novelist and one of her greatest poets
—troubled himself to demonstrate in his *Storia della Colonna
Infame.* Illustrating at length a passage on torture in his novel
I Promessi Sposi, Manzoni acknowledges that Beccaria's "little
book, which was rather an overflow of spontaneous inspirations
than a work of premeditated study, prompted, and I am on
the verge of saying, commanded the reform" of criminal law.[28]
But then he proceeds to review the evidence marshalled in
justification of its severe indictment of the past. For that purpose he examines Pietro Verri's *Osservazioni sulla Tortura,*
posthumously published in 1804,[29] in which one may read for
oneself the materials that were drummed into Beccaria's ears
when Verri was priming him to write on crimes and punishments.

Manzoni stresses particularly the misrepresentation of the
juridical ideas of the preceding ages, defending at length the
jurists Claro and Farinacci, who are so pointedly maligned in
the opening paragraphs of Beccaria's treatise. He shows that
Verri, followed by Beccaria, attributed to them doctrines the
very opposite of what they taught. He observes that they were,
in fact, men no less compassionate than the humanitarian rationalists who criticized them; that they had labored long, not
merely with words, but with the full weight of their juridical
authority, to check the ever-lively tendency of law-enforcers to
apply inordinate physical and psychological pressures in their

[28] Alessandro Manzoni, *Tutte le Opere di Alessandro Manzoni,* ed.
Alberto Chiari and Fausto Ghisalberti (Milan, 1959), II¹, 969.

[29] Pietro Verri, *Osservazioni Sulla Tortura,* in *Scrittori Classici Italiani
di Economia Politica,* Parte Moderna (Milan, 1804), XVII, 191-319.

efforts to maintain public order. In language permeated by the "historical spirit," defended by Frederic Maitland, Manzoni thus places the radical reform movement in historical perspective:

> That is how it usually happens with human reforms which are only gradually accomplished (I speak of genuine and just reforms, not of all things that have taken the name): to the men who first undertake them, it seems a great deal to modify the situation, to correct it in various parts, to subtract and add. Those who come later, often much later, finding the situation still bad (as it is), are likely to dwell on the latest contributors, condemning as authors those whose names are most recently connected with it, simply because they have given it the form in which it currently lives and prevails.[30]

Beccaria, according to Manzoni, was one of those who came much later. Having exaggerated the number and strength of his enemies, he was filled with wonder, understandably, at the apparent efficacy of his words. But students of history ought not to perpetuate his exaggerations, for it is simply not true that the criminal procedures Beccaria attacked were as vicious as he made them out to be; neither is it true that the system of law he boldly challenged "had on its side," as some of his admirers assert, "all authority living and dead." Old, and undermined in many parts as it was, that husk of ancient law "would have fallen eventually," so Manzoni concludes, "even under the blows of less spirited assailants. . . . But at an earlier time such a triumph would have been impossible: in the vigor of youth, error is stronger than genius." [31]

NOTE ON THE TEXT. This translation of *Dei Delitti e delle Pene* is based primarily upon the Italian text in Cesare Beccaria, *Opere*, edited by Sergio Romagnoli (Florence, 1958), I, 35-133. For the history of the text and an extensive bibliography, see *Opere*, I, xcix-cix, and II, 917-18.

HENRY PAOLUCCI

---

[30] Manzoni, *Opere*, II¹, 695.
[31] *Ibid.*, II³, 683.

ON CRIMES AND
PUNISHMENTS

In all negotiations of difficulty, a
man may not look to sow and reap
at once, but must prepare business,
and so ripen it by degrees.

BACON

[Essay XLVII,
"Of Negotiating"]

TO THE READER

A few remnants of the laws of an ancient predatory people, compiled for a monarch who ruled twelve centuries ago in Constantinople,[1] mixed subsequently with Longobardic tribal customs,[2] and bound together in the chaotic volumes of obscure and unauthorized interpreters—these form the tradition of opinions which in a large part of Europe is still accorded the name of law. And it is as deplorable as it is common in our own day that an opinion of Carpzov,[3] an ancient usage cited by Claro,[4] a torture suggested with irritating complacency by Farinacci,[5] should make up the laws accepted with confidence by those who ought, only with trembling diffidence, to govern

1 [Under Justinian I, Byzantine Emperor (527-565 A.D.), the great *Corpus Juris Civilis* was compiled by a committee of Roman jurists headed by Tribonian. Its four parts are the *Code* (a collection of imperial constitutions), the *Digest* (a selection from the writings of elder Roman jurists), the *Institutes* (an introductory treatise), and the *Novellae* (imperial constitutions issued by Justinian I after 534).]

2 [The Germanic Longobards invaded Italy in 568 A.D., establishing centers of domination at Pavia, Spoleto, and Benevento. Their customary law was codified, after their conversion to Christianity, in the *Edictum Rotharis* (643 A.D.).]

3 [Benedikt Carpzov (1595-1666), jurist of Leipzig. His scholarly work and official practice were of fundamental importance in systematizing the various Saxon, Roman, and Canon law elements that make up the body of Germanic law. Most significant for criminal law is his *Practica nova imperialis saxonica rerum criminalium* (1635).]

4 [Giulio Claro (Latin, Clarus: 1525-1575), criminologist. He studied law at Pavia and Bologna, and served, under Philip II, as head of the Supreme Italian Council in Madrid. His chief work is the *Receptae sententiae* (1570), the last part of which treats of criminal law.]

5 [Prospero Farinacci (Latin, Farinacius: 1544-1618), penologist. A brilliant advocate, he later served as procurator-general under Pope Paul V. He undertook to systematize the juridical opinions of the great line of jurists that began with the Bolognese civilists and canonists of the twelfth and thirteenth centuries. His chief work is the series of volumes *Praxis et theorica criminalis*, publication of which began in 1588.]

3

the lives and fortunes of men. These laws, the dregs of utterly barbarous centuries, are examined in this book with regard only for the part that relates to the criminal system; needless to say it is only for the sake of the directors of the public welfare, and in a style designed to ward off the unenlightened and excitable masses, that we presume to exhibit their disorders here. The frank searching out of truth, the freedom from commonplace opinions which characterize this book are consequences of the benevolence and enlightenment of the government under which the author lives. The great monarchs, the benefactors of humanity who rule us, are pleased to hear truths expounded, even by an unknown thinker, not fanatically, but with a zeal aroused solely by those who, repulsed by reason, vent themselves in violence and cunning; the current disorders will appear, upon thorough examination of the circumstances, to be a satire and reproach of ages past and not of this century and its lawgivers.

Whoever might wish to honor me with his criticism should therefore begin by understanding clearly the design of this work, a design which, far from diminishing legitimate authority, must serve to increase it, if reasoning rather than force can prevail among men, and if benevolence and humanity justify it in the eyes of all. The mistaken criticisms published against this book [first edition] [6] are founded upon confused notions, and they oblige me to interrupt for a moment my discourse with enlightened readers in order once and forever to preclude all access to the errors of a timorous zeal, or to the calumnies of malicious envy.

The moral and political principles that govern men derive from three sources: revelation, natural law, and the established conventions of society. Regarding its ultimate end, the first is

[6] [This prefatory "To the Reader" first appeared in the second edition. Among the chief criticisms provoked by the first edition was a work entitled *Note ed osservazioni sul libro intitolato Dei delitti e delle pene* (1765), by Angelo Fachinei, a Dominican monk who wrote under the auspices of the Venetian Republic.]

beyond comparison with the others: but they are alike in this, that all three lead to happiness in this mortal life. To consider the relations of the third is not to exclude the relations of the first two. Rather, for the very reason that these, despite their divine and immutable character, have suffered thousands of changes effected by false religions and by arbitrary notions of vice and virtue for which men themselves are to blame, it seems a matter of necessity to examine, apart from every other consideration, the products of purely human convention, expressly formulated or assumed for the need and advantage of society —an idea with which every sect and every moral system is bound to concur. And it will always be a praiseworthy undertaking which serves to constrain even the most headstrong and skeptical to conform to the principles that prompt men to live in society. There are, then, three distinct classes of virtue and of vice: religious, natural, and political. These three classes ought never to be in contradiction, but the consequences and duties deriving from one are not all derivable also from the others. Natural law by no means enjoins all that revelation enjoins, nor does the purely social law enjoin all that is enjoined by the natural. But it is of utmost importance to distinguish what results from convention, that is, from the expressed or tacit compacts of men, for therein lies the limit of the power that can legitimately be exercised by one man over another, without a special mandate from the Supreme Being. The idea of political virtue may, thus, without reproach, be termed variable; the idea of natural virtue would ever remain clear and obvious, were it not obscured by the stupidities and passions of men; the idea of religious virtue does, indeed, remain one and the same, because it is directly revealed by God, and is by Him sustained.

It would be a mistake, therefore, to ascribe to one who speaks of social conventions and their consequences principles contrary either to natural law or revelation, for he does not speak of these. It would be a mistake, also, when the assertion is made that a state of war preceded the formation of so-

ciety, to take it in the Hobbesian sense,[7] as admitting no
anterior duty and obligation, instead of taking it simply as
a fact arising from the corruption of human nature and from
the absence of an explicit sanction. It would be a mistake,
when an author is considering the results of the social contract, to find fault with him for not admitting the existence of
duty and obligation prior to the pact itself.[8]

Divine justice and natural justice are of their very essence
immutable and abiding, for the relation between things that
remain the same is ever the same. But human, or rather political, justice, being merely the relation between a given action
and the ever varying condition of society, is subject to change
to the extent that the action in question may become necessary or useful to society; nor is it readily discernible except by
one who analyzes the complex and ever changing relations of
civic associations. Once these essentially distinct principles are
confounded, there can be no further hope of correct reasoning in public affairs. It pertains to theologians to determine
the boundaries between the just and the unjust with regard
to the intrinsic wickedness or goodness of an act; to determine
the relations of the politically just and unjust pertains to the
statesman. Nor can the object aimed at by one prejudice the
other, since it is apparent to all to what extent purely political
virtue ought to yield to the immutable virtue that emanates
from God.

Whoever, I repeat, might wish to honor me with his criti-

---

[7] [Thomas Hobbes (1588-1679). The Hobbesian doctrines of a primitive
state of universal warfare (*bellum omnium contra omnes*) and of the
mutual transferring of right which terminates that warfare are developed
primarily in *Leviathan* (originally published, 1651), Part One, chaps. 13
and 14. See the Library of Liberal Arts edition, No. 69 (New York, 1958),
pp. 104-19.]

[8] [The idea that political community is based, either historically or
theoretically, on a "social contract" into which men enter in order to
facilitate their pursuit of happiness is at least as old as the Greek Sophists
and their Epicurean successors. Hobbes, Locke, and Rousseau were
Beccaria's sources—though his utilitarian emphasis owes less to these three
than to Helvetius' *De l'esprit* (1758).]

cism ought not to begin, therefore, by attributing to me principles that subvert virtue and religion, for I have demonstrated that I hold no such principles. Instead of representing me as an unbeliever or revolutionary, let him rather try to prove me a bad logician or a short-sighted political theorist; but let him not tremble at every utterance that upholds the interests of mankind. Let him persuade me of the uselessness of my principles or of the political harm that might arise from them; let him show me the advantages of the accepted practices. I have given public testimony of my religion and of obedience to my sovereign in my reply [9] to the "Notes and Observations"; to reply to further queries of the same order would be superfluous. But any person disposed to write with the decorum expected of honorable men, and with sufficient intelligence not to require of me that I prove my first principles, whatever they may be, will find in me not so much a man eager to reply as a steadfast lover of truth.

I

INTRODUCTION

Men generally abandon the most important regulations either to the care of ordinary common sense or to the discretion of persons who have an interest in opposing the wisest laws—laws, that is, of the kind that naturally promote the universal distribution of advantages while they resist the force that tends to concentrate them in the hands of a few, placing the summit of power and happiness on one side, and on the other, only weakness and misery. It is, therefore, only after they have passed through a thousand errors in matters most

9 [This reply to Fachinei's attacks was published anonymously at Lucerne in 1765 under the title *Risposta ad uno scritto che s'intitola "Note ed osservazioni sul libro* Dei delitti e delle pene." Though Beccaria here claims it as his own, there is no doubt that it was actually written in his behalf by Pietro and Alessandro Verri.]

essential to life and liberty, after they have arrived at the limits of endurance, exhausted by the wrongs they have suffered, that men are induced to remedy the disorders that oppress them and to acknowledge the most palpable truths, which, precisely because of their simplicity, escape the attention of vulgar minds accustomed not to analyzing things, but to receiving general impressions all of a piece, rather from tradition than through study.

If we glance at the pages of history, we will find that laws, which surely are, or ought to be, compacts of free men, have been, for the most part, a mere tool of the passions of some, or have arisen from an accidental and temporary need. Never have they been dictated by a dispassionate student of human nature who might, by bringing the actions of a multitude of men into focus, consider them from this single point of view: the *greatest happiness shared by the greatest number*.[10] Happy are those few nations that have not waited for the slow succession of coincidence and human vicissitude to force some little turn for the better after the limit of evil has been reached, but have facilitated the intermediate progress by means of good laws. And humanity owes a debt of gratitude to that philosopher who, from the obscurity of his isolated study, had the courage to scatter among the multitude the first seeds, so long unfruitful, of useful truths.[11]

The true relations between sovereigns and their subjects, and between nations, have been discovered. Commerce has been reanimated by the common knowledge of philosophical truths diffused by the art of printing, and there has sprung up among nations a tacit rivalry of industriousness that is most humane and truly worthy of rational beings. Such good things we owe to the productive enlightenment of this age. But very

---

[10] ["La massima felicità divisa nel maggior numero." Many approximations of this celebrated formula are no doubt to be found in the extensive literature of eudaimonistic and hedonistic ethics which originated with the ancient Greeks, but there is no question that Jeremy Bentham, who made the formula famous, first encountered it here.]

[11] [Perhaps Jean Jacques Rousseau.]

few persons have studied and fought against the cruelty of punishments and the irregularities of criminal procedures, a part of legislation that is as fundamental as it is widely neglected in almost all of Europe. Very few persons have undertaken to demolish the accumulated errors of centuries by rising to general principles, curbing, at least, with the sole force that acknowledged truths possess, the unbounded course of ill-directed power which has continually produced a long and authorized example of the most cold-blooded barbarity. And yet the groans of the weak, sacrificed to cruel ignorance and to opulent indolence; the barbarous torments, multiplied with lavish and useless severity, for crimes either not proved or wholly imaginary; the filth and horrors of a prison, intensified by that cruellest tormentor of the miserable, uncertainty—all these ought to have roused that breed of magistrates who direct the opinions of men.

The immortal Montesquieu [12] has cursorily touched upon this subject. Truth, which is one and indivisible, has obliged me to follow the illustrious steps of that great man, but the thoughtful men for whom I write will easily distinguish my traces from his. I shall deem myself happy if I can obtain, as he did, the secret thanks of the unknown and peace-loving disciples of reason, and if I can inspire that tender thrill with which persons of sensibility respond to one who upholds the interests of humanity.

Adherence to a strictly logical sequence would now lead us to examine and distinguish the various kinds of crimes and modes of punishment; but these are by their nature so variable, because of the diverse circumstances of time and place, that the result would be a catalogue of enormous and boring detail. By indicating only the most general principles and the

12 [Charles Louis de Secondat, Baron de la Brède et de Montesquieu (1689-1755). Beccaria was greatly excited and influenced by Montesquieu's *Persian Letters* (1721) and *The Spirit of the Laws* (1748). Book XI of the latter work has been called "the Magna Carta of criminals." See Franz Neumann's Introduction to *The Spirit of the Laws* (New York, 1949), p. 1.]

most dangerous and commonest errors, I will have done
enough to disabuse both those who, from a mistaken love of
liberty, would be ready to introduce anarchy, and those who
would like to see all men subjected to a monastic discipline.
   But what are to be the proper punishments for such crimes?
Is the death-penalty really *useful* and *necessary* for the security and good order of society? Are torture and torments *just*,
and do they attain the *end* for which laws are instituted? What
is the best way to prevent crimes? Are the same punishments
equally effective for all times? What influence have they on
customary behavior? These problems deserve to be analyzed
with that geometric precision which the mist of sophisms, seductive eloquence, and timorous doubt cannot withstand. If I
could boast only of having been the first to present to Italy,
with a little more clarity, what other nations have boldly written and are beginning to practice, I would account myself
fortunate. But if, by defending the rights of man and of unconquerable truth, I should help to save from the spasm and
agonies of death some wretched victim of tyranny or of no less
fatal ignorance, the thanks and tears of one innocent mortal
in his transports of joy would console me for the contempt of
all mankind.

II

THE ORIGIN OF PUNISHMENTS, AND THE RIGHT TO PUNISH

   No lasting advantage is to be hoped for from political
morality if it is not founded upon the ineradicable feelings of
mankind. Any law that deviates from these will inevitably encounter a resistance that is certain to prevail over it in the end
—in the same way that any force, however small, if continu-
ously applied, is bound to overcome the most violent motion
that can be imparted to a body.
   Let us consult the human heart, and we shall find there the

basic principles of the true right of the sovereign to punish crimes.

No man ever freely sacrificed a portion of his personal liberty merely in behalf of the common good. That chimera exists only in romances. If it were possible, every one of us would prefer that the compacts binding others did not bind us; every man tends to make himself the center of his whole world.[13]

The continuous multiplication of mankind, inconsiderable in itself yet exceeding by far the means that a sterile and uncultivated nature could offer for the satisfaction of increasingly complex needs, united the earliest savages. These first communities of necessity caused the formation of others to resist the first, and the primitive state of warfare thus passed from individuals to nations.[14]

Laws are the conditions under which independent and isolated men united to form a society. Weary of living in a continual state of war, and of enjoying a liberty rendered useless by the uncertainty of preserving it, they sacrificed a part so that they might enjoy the rest of it in peace and safety.[15] The

13 [This negative view of the political constitution of society as a mere restriction on individual liberty, to be endured as a necessary evil, is, of course, apparently consistent with Rousseau's statement of the "fundamental problem" of the *Social Contract* (I, 6), which is "to find a form of association which will defend and protect the person and property of each associate, and wherein each member, united to all the others, still obeys himself alone, and retains his original freedom."]

14 [See Montesquieu, *Spirit of the Laws*, I, ii-iii: "Hobbes inquires, 'For what reason go men armed, and have locks and keys to fasten their doors, if they be not naturally in a state of war?' But is it not obvious that he attributes to mankind before the establishment of society what can happen but in consequence of this establishment, which furnishes them with motives for hostile attacks and self-defense? . . . As soon as man enters into a state of society he loses the sense of his weakness; equality ceases, and then commences the state of war."]

15 [Cf. Plato, *Republic* III: "When men have both done and suffered injustice they think they had better agree among themselves. . . . Hence there arise laws and mutual covenants." See also Lucretius, *De Rerum Natura* V. 1135ff.: "Affairs sank down to turmoil's lowest dregs, when each one was seeking for himself supremacy and highest place. Then some advised appointing magistrates, and drew up codes, that men might wish

sum of all these portions of liberty sacrificed by each for his own good constitutes the sovereignty of a nation, and their legitimate depositary and administrator is the sovereign. But merely to have established this deposit was not enough; it had to be defended against private usurpations by individuals each of whom always tries not only to withdraw his own share but also to usurp for himself that of others. Some tangible motives had to be introduced, therefore, to prevent the despotic spirit, which is in every man, from plunging the laws of society into its original chaos. These tangible motives are the punishments established against infractors of the laws. I say "tangible motives" because experience has shown that the multitude adopt no fixed principles of conduct and will not be released from the sway of that universal principle of dissolution which is seen to operate both in the physical and the moral universe, except for motives that directly strike the senses. These motives, by dint of repeated representation to the mind, counterbalance the powerful impressions of the private passions that oppose the common good.[16] Not eloquence, not declamations, not even the most sublime truths have sufficed, for any considerable length of time, to curb passions excited by vivid impressions of present objects.

It was, thus, necessity that forced men to give up part of their personal liberty, and it is certain, therefore, that each is willing to place in the public fund only the least possible por-

deterrence? (handwritten margin note)

---

to have the use of laws; because mankind, worn out with living lives of violence, lay languishing from feuds; wherefore the more spontaneously they gave submission to strict codes of law."]

16 [For a critique of this utilitarian concept of the "right" of punishment, see G. W. F. Hegel's *Philosophy of Right*, tr. T. M. Knox, (Oxford, 1942), pp. 69-73 and 246-47. According to Hegel, the use of punishment as a deterrent, or preventive "threat," cannot be justified in the political association of free and equal human beings. "To base a justification of punishment on threat," Hegel writes, "is to liken it to the act of a man who lifts his stick to a dog. It is to treat a man like a dog instead of with the freedom and respect due to him as a man. But a threat, which after all may rouse a man to demonstrate his freedom in spite of it, discards justice altogether" (p. 246).]

tion, no more than suffices to induce others to defend it.[17] The aggregate of these least possible portions constitutes the right to punish; all that exceeds this is abuse and not justice; it is fact but by no means right.[18]

Punishments that exceed what is necessary for protection of the deposit of public security are by their very nature unjust, and punishments are increasingly more just as the safety which the sovereign secures for his subjects is the more sacred and inviolable, and the liberty greater.[19]

What about retribution? (margin note)

III

CONSEQUENCES

The first consequence of these principles is that only the laws can decree punishments for crimes; authority for this can reside only with the legislator who represents the entire so-

17 [Cf. Rousseau, *Social Contract*, II, 4: "It is granted that all which an individual alienates by the social compact is only that part of his power, his property, and his liberty, the use of which is important to the community; but we must also grant that the sovereign is the only judge of what is important to the community."]

18 Note that the word "right" is not opposed to the word "might"; the first is rather a modification of the second—that modification, to be precise, which is most advantageous to the greater number. And by "justice" I mean nothing more than the bond required to maintain the unity of particular interests which would otherwise dissolve into the original state of insociability.

Care must be taken not to attach to this word "justice" the idea of some real thing, as of a physical force or of an existent being; it is simply a human way of conceiving things, a way that has an enormous influence on everyone's happiness. Much less have I in mind that other kind of justice which emanates from God, and which relates directly to the punishments and rewards of the life to come.

19 [Cf. Aristotle, *Politics* VII. 13: "Just punishments and chastisements do indeed spring from a good principle, but they are good only because we cannot do without them—it would be better that neither individuals nor states should need anything of the sort."]

ciety united by a social contract. No magistrate (who is a part
of society) can, with justice, inflict punishments upon another
member of the same society. But a punishment that exceeds
the limit fixed by the laws is just punishment plus another
punishment; a magistrate cannot, therefore, under any pretext
of zeal or concern for the public good, augment the punishment established for a delinquent citizen.

The second consequence is that the sovereign, who represents
the society itself, can frame only general laws binding all members, but he cannot judge whether someone has violated the
social contract, for that would divide the nation into two
parts, one represented by the sovereign, who asserts the violation of the contract, and the other by the accused, who denies it. There must, therefore, be a third party to judge the
truth of the fact. Hence the need for a magistrate whose de-
cisions, from which there can be no appeal, should consist of
mere affirmations or denials of particular facts.

The third consequence is this: even assuming that severity of
punishments were not directly contrary to the public good
and to the very purpose of preventing crimes, if it were possible to prove merely that such severity is useless, in that case
also it would be contrary not only to those beneficent virtues
that spring from enlightened reason which would rather rule
happy men than a herd of slaves in whom a timid cruelty
makes its endless rounds; it would be contrary to justice itself
and to the very nature of the social contract.

IV

INTERPRETATIONS OF THE LAWS

A fourth consequence: Judges in criminal cases cannot have
the authority to interpret laws, and the reason, again, is that
they are not legislators. Such judges have not received the laws
from our ancestors as a family tradition or legacy that leaves
to posterity only the burden of obeying them, but they receive

them, rather, from the living society, or from the sovereign representing it, who is the legitimate depositary of what actually results from the common will of all. [The judges] receive them not as obligations of some ancient oath [20] (null, to begin with, because it pretended to bind wills that were not then existent, and iniquitous, because it reduced men from a social state to that of an animal herd), but as consequences of the tacit or expressed oath of allegiance which the united wills of living subjects have pledged to their sovereign, as bonds necessary for restraining and regulating the internal ferment of private interests. This constitutes the natural and real authority of the laws. Who, then, is to be the legitimate interpreter of the laws? Is it to be the sovereign, that is, the depositary of the actual wills of all, or the judge, whose sole charge is merely to examine whether a particular man has or has not committed an unlawful act?

For every crime that comes before him, a judge is required to complete a perfect syllogism in which the major premise must be the general law; the minor, the action that conforms or does not conform to the law; and the conclusion, acquittal or punishment. If the judge were constrained, or if he desired to frame even a single additional syllogism, the door would thereby be opened to uncertainty.

Nothing can be more dangerous than the popular axiom that it is necessary to consult the spirit of the laws. It is a dam that has given way to a torrent of opinions. This truth, which seems paradoxical to ordinary minds that are struck more by

[20] Each individual is indeed bound to society, but society is, in turn, bound to each individual by a contract which, of its very nature, places both parties under obligation. This obligation, which descends from the throne to the cottage, which binds equally the loftiest and the meanest of men, signifies only that it is in the interests of all that the pacts advantageous to the greatest number be observed.

The word "obligation" is one of those that occur much more frequently in ethics than in any other science, and which are the abbreviated symbol of a rational argument and not of an idea. Seek an adequate idea of the word "obligation" and you will fail to find it; reason about it and you will both understand yourself and be understood by others.

trivial present disorders than by the dangerous but remote effects of false principles rooted in a nation, seems to me to be fully demonstrated. Our understandings and all our ideas have a reciprocal connection; the more complicated they are, the more numerous must the ways be that lead to them and depart from them. Each man has his own point of view, and, at each different time, a different one. Thus the "spirit" of the law would be the product of a judge's good or bad logic, of his good or bad digestion; it would depend on the violence of his passions, on the weakness of the accused, on the judge's connections with him, and on all those minute factors that alter the appearances of an object in the fluctuating mind of man. Thus we see the lot of a citizen subjected to frequent changes in passing through different courts, and we see the lives of poor wretches become the victims of the false ratiocinations or of the momentary seething ill-humors of a judge who mistakes for a legitimate interpretation that vague product of the jumbled series of notions which his mind stirs up. Thus we see the same crimes differently punished at different times by the same court, for having consulted not the constant fixed voice of the law but the erring instability of interpretation.

The disorder that arises from rigorous observance of the letter of a penal law is hardly comparable to the disorders that arise from interpretations. The temporary inconvenience of the former prompts one to make the rather easy and needed correction in the words of the law which are the source of uncertainty, but it curbs that fatal license of discussion which gives rise to arbitrary and venal controversies. When a fixed code of laws, which must be observed to the letter, leaves no further care to the judge than to examine the acts of citizens and to decide whether or not they conform to the law as written; when the standard of the just or the unjust, which is to be the norm of conduct for the ignorant as well as for the philosophic citizen, is not a matter of controversy but of fact; then only are citizens not subject to the petty tyrannies of the many which are the more cruel as the distance between the oppressed and the oppressor is less, and which are far more fatal than those of a single man, for the despotism of many can only be corrected by the despotism of one; the cruelty of a single despot is proportioned, not to his might, but to the obstacles he encounters. In this way citizens acquire that sense of security for their own persons which is just, because it is the object of human association, and useful, because it enables them to calculate accurately the inconveniences of a misdeed. It is true, also, that they acquire a spirit of independence, but not one that upsets the laws and resists the chief magistrates; rather one that resists those who have dared to apply the sacred name of virtue to that weakness of theirs which makes them yield to their self-interested and capricious opinions.

These principles will displease those who have assumed for themselves a right to transmit to their inferiors the blows of tyranny that they have received from their superiors. I would, indeed, be most fearful if the spirit of tyranny were in the least compatible with the spirit of literacy.

V

OBSCURITY OF THE LAWS

If the interpretation of laws is an evil, another evil, evidently, is the obscurity that makes interpretation necessary. And this evil would be very great indeed where the laws are written in a language that is foreign to a people, forcing it to rely on a handful of men because it is unable to judge for itself how its liberty or its members may fare—in a language that transforms a sacred and public book into something very like the private possession of a family. When the number of those who can understand the sacred code of laws and hold it in their hands increases, the frequency of crimes will be found to decrease, for undoubtedly ignorance and uncertainty of punishments add much to the eloquence of the passions. What are we to make of men, therefore, when we reflect that this very evil is the inveterate practice of a large part of cultured and enlightened Europe?

One consequence of this last reflection is that, without writing, a society can never acquire a fixed form of government with power that derives from the whole and not from the parts, in which the laws, which cannot be altered except by the general will, are not corrupted in their passage through the mass of private interests. Experience and reason have shown us that the probability and certainty of human traditions diminish the further removed they are from their source. For, obviously, if there exists no enduring memorial of the social compact, how are the laws to withstand the inevitable pressure of time and of passions?

We can thus see how useful the art of printing is, which makes the public, and not some few individuals, the guardians of the sacred laws. And we can see how it has dissipated the benighted spirit of cabal and intrigue, which must soon vanish in the presence of those enlightened studies and sciences, apparently despised, but really feared, by its adherents. This explains why we now see in Europe a diminishing of the atrocity of the crimes that afflicted our ancestors, who became tyrants and slaves by turns. Any one acquainted with the history of the past two centuries, and of our own time, may observe how from the lap of luxury and softness have sprung the most pleasing virtues, humanity, benevolence, and toleration of human errors. He will see what the real effects were of the so-called simplicity and good faith of old: humanity groaning under implacable superstition; avarice and private ambition staining with blood the golden treasure-chests and thrones of kings; secret betrayals and public massacres; every nobleman a tyrant over the people; ministers of the Gospel truth polluting with blood the hands that daily touched the God of mercy—these, surely, are not the work of this enlightened age that some people call corrupt.

VI

IMPRISONMENT

An error no less common than it is contrary to the purpose
of association—which is assurance of personal security—is that
of allowing a magistrate charged with administering the laws
to be free to imprison a citizen at his own pleasure, to deprive
an enemy of liberty on frivolous pretexts, and to leave a friend
unpunished notwithstanding the clearest evidences of his guilt.
Detention in prison is a punishment which, unlike every other,
must of necessity precede conviction for crime, but this distinctive character does not remove the other which is essential—
namely, that only the law determines the cases in which a man
is to suffer punishment. It pertains to the law, therefore, to
indicate what evidences of crime justify detention of the accused, his subjection to investigation and punishment. A man's
notoriety, his flight, his nonjudicial confession, the confession
of an accomplice, threats and the constant enmity of the injured person, the manifest fact of the crime, and similar evidences, are proofs sufficient to justify imprisonment of a citizen.
But these proofs must be determined by the law, not by judges,
whose decrees are always contrary to political liberty when they
are not particular applications of a general maxim included
in the public code. When punishments have become more
moderate, when squalor and hunger have been removed from
prisons, when pity and mercy have forced a way through
barred doors, overmastering the inexorable and obdurate
ministers of justice, then may the laws be content with slighter
evidences as grounds for imprisonment.

A man accused of a crime, who has been imprisoned and
acquitted, ought not to be branded with infamy. How many
Romans accused of very great crimes, and then found innocent,
were revered by the populace and honored with public offices!
For what reason, then, is the fate of an innocent person so apt
to be different in our time? It seems to be because, in the pres-

ent system of criminal law, the idea of power and arrogance prevails over that of justice, because accused and convicted are thrown indiscriminately into the same cell, because imprisonment is rather the torment than the confinement of the accused, and because the internal power that protects the laws and the external power that defends the throne and nation are separated when they ought to be united. By means of the common sanction of the laws, the former [internal power] would be combined with judicial authority, without, however, passing directly under its sway; the glory that attends the pomp and ceremony of a military corps would remove infamy, which, like all popular sentiments, is more attached to the manner than to the thing itself, as is proved by the fact that military prisons are, according to the common opinion, less disgraceful than the civil. Still discernible in our people, in their customs and laws, which always lag several ages behind the actual enlightened thought of a nation—still discernible are the barbaric impressions and savage notions of those people of the North who hunted down our forefathers.

VII

EVIDENCES AND FORMS OF JUDGMENTS

There is a general theorem that is very useful in calculating the certainty of a fact, as, for example, the weight of evidences of a crime. When proofs of a fact are dependent one on another, that is, when the evidences depend on themselves for proof, the more proofs adduced, the less probable the fact, because the circumstances that might make the first proofs defective would make all subsequent ones equally defective. When all the proofs of a fact depend equally on a single one, the number of proofs neither increases nor decreases the probability of the fact, for their entire force resolves itself into the force of that single one on which they depend. When the proofs are independent of each other, that is, when the evidences are proved otherwise than through themselves, the more proofs adduced, the greater the certainty of the fact, for the falsity of one proof will not affect the other. I speak of probability, here, with respect to crimes, when it would seem that certainty is demanded if they are to deserve punishment. But the paradox will vanish if one considers that, strictly speaking, moral certainty is never more than a probability, but a probability that is called certainty, because every man of good sense naturally gives his assent to it by force of a habit which arises from the necessity to act and is anterior to all speculation. The certainty required to prove a man guilty, therefore, is that which determines every man in the most important transactions of his life.

The proofs of a crime can be distinguished as perfect and imperfect. Perfect I call those that exclude the possibility of innocence; imperfect, those that do not exclude it. Of the first, a single one suffices for condemnation; of the second, as many are necessary as suffice to form a single perfect one; in other words, such that, though each separately does not exclude the possibility of innocence, their convergence on the same subject makes innocence an impossibility. One should note, however, that imperfect proofs of which the accused could clear himself, but does not, become perfect. But this moral certainty of proof is more easily felt than exactly defined. That is why I consider an excellent law that which assigns popular jurors, taken by lot, to assist the chief judge, for in this case ignorance judging on feeling is more reliable than science judging on opinion. Where laws are clear and precise, a judge's duty is merely to ascertain the fact. If, in searching out proofs of a crime, ability and dexterity are required, if clarity and precision are necessary in presenting the result, in forming a judgment on the result itself, all that is required is ordinary good sense, less fallacious, surely, than the learning of the judge, long used to finding men guilty, who always seeks to reduce things to an artificial system borrowed from his studies. Happy the nation where the laws need not be a science! Most useful is the law that each man ought to be judged by his peers, for, where it

is a matter of the liberty or the fortune of a citizen, the feelings which inequality inspires should be silent; neither the
superiority with which the prosperous man regards the unfortunate, nor the disdain with which the inferior regards his
superior, can have any place in this judgment. But when a
crime involves injury to a fellow citizen, then the judges ought
to be peers, half of the accused, half of the injured. In this way,
by carefully balancing every private concern that might even
involuntarily transform the aspect of things, nothing is heard
to speak but the laws and the truth. It also accords with justice
to permit the accused to refuse, on suspicion, a certain number of his judges; when this opportunity has been allowed him
for a time, without opposition, the accused will seem almost
to condemn himself. Let the verdicts and proofs of guilt be
made public, so that opinion, which is, perhaps, the sole cement of society, may serve to restrain power and passions; so
that the people may say, we are not slaves, and we are protected—a sentiment which inspires courage and which is the
equivalent of a tribute to a sovereign who knows his own true
interests. I shall not enter upon other specific points and pre-
cautions requiring similar regulations. I should have said
nothing, were it necessary to say all.

VIII

WITNESSES

It is a considerable point in all good legislation to determine
exactly the credibility of witnesses and the proofs of a crime.
Every reasonable man, everyone, that is, whose ideas have a certain interconnection and whose feelings accord with those of
other men, may be a witness. The true measure of his credibility is nothing other than his interest in telling or in not telling the truth; for this reason it is frivolous to insist that women
are too weak [to be good witnesses], childish to insist that civil
death in a condemned man has the same effects as real death,

and meaningless to insist on the infamy of the infamous, when they have no interest in lying.

Noteworthy among the other abuses of language, which have more than a little influenced human affairs, is the one that renders null and void the deposition of a condemned criminal. He is *civilly dead,* say the peripatetic jurists, and a *dead man* is incapable of any action. To sustain this empty metaphor, numerous victims have been sacrificed, and it has often been disputed, in serious discourse, whether truth should not be made to yield to judicial formulas. So long as the depositions of a condemned criminal are not such as to arrest the course of justice, why not allow him, even after conviction, both as a concession to his extreme misery and in the interests of truth, a suitable period of time so that, by introducing fresh evidences sufficient to alter the nature of the fact, he may justify himself, or another, in a new trial? Formalities and ceremonies are necessary in the administration of justice, not only because they leave nothing to be determined arbitrarily by the administrator, and because they give the populace the impression of a judgment that is not rash and partisan, but stable and regular; but also because, on men who are imitators and slaves of custom, things which impress the senses make a more lasting impression than rational arguments. But it is never without fatal danger to fix such formalities by law so firmly as to make them injurious to truth, which, whether because it is too simple or too complex, has need of some external pomp to conciliate the ignorant populace. The credibility of a witness, therefore, must diminish in proportion to the hatred, or friendship, or close connections between him and the accused. More than one witness is necessary, for, so long as one affirms and the other denies, nothing is certain, and the right of every man to be presumed innocent prevails. The credibility of a witness becomes appreciably less, the greater the atrocity of the crime [21]

[21] According to the criminalists, the credibility of a witness increases with the atrocity of the crime. Behold the iron maxim which cruelest imbecility dictates: "In atrocissimis leviores coniecturae sufficiunt, et licet judici jura transgredi." Let us translate this into ordinary language and

or the improbability of the circumstances. Witchcraft and
deeds of wanton cruelty are instances. With regard to the first
of these, the probability is greater that many are apt to lie, because it is far more likely that an illusion shaped by ignorance
and by persecuting hatred should arise in many men than that
one man should exercise a power which God either has given
to none or has taken from every created being. The same is
true with regard to the second [deeds of wanton cruelty], for
man is never cruel except in proportion to the personal interest, hatred, or fear he conceives. Strictly speaking there can
be no superfluous feeling in man; there is always an exact
accord with the result of impressions made on the senses. Similarly the credibility of a witness is sometimes diminished if he
happens to be a member of a secret society, the customs and
principles of which are either not well understood or different
from those of the public. Such a man has his own passions
and those of others as well.

Almost null, finally, is the credibility of a witness when a
crime is made to depend on words. The tone, the gesture, all
that precedes or follows the different ideas men attach to the
same words—these so alter and modify the utterances of a man
that it is almost impossible to repeat them precisely as they

---

enable all Europeans to see one of the very many equally senseless maxims
of those to whom, almost without being aware of it, they are subject: "In
the most atrocious crimes (that is, in the least likely) the slightest conjectures suffice, and the judge is authorized to exceed the law." The absurdities of legal practice are the products of fear, which is the chief source
of human contradictions. Legislators (such are the jurists whom chance
has authorized to decide concerning all things, to become, after having
been interested and venal writers, arbiters and legislators of the fortunes
of men), frightened by the condemnation of some innocent person, burden
jurisprudence with superfluous formalities and exceptions, strict observance of which would enable anarchy to sit with impunity upon the throne
of justice. Frightened by some not easily proved and atrocious crimes,
they imagine themselves obliged to disregard the very formalities they
have established; and so, now with despotic impatience, now with effeminate trepidation, they transform grave trials into a kind of game in
which hazard and deception are the chief players.

were said.[22] Moreover, actions that are violent and extraordinary leave traces in a multitude of circumstances and in the effects that flow from them; with regard to these, the greater the number adduced in proof, the more numerous the means enabling the accused to clear himself. But words remain only in the memory of the listeners, which is, for the most part, untrustworthy and easily deceived. It is for that reason easier to attack a man's words with calumny than his actions.

IX

SECRET ACCUSATIONS

Evident, but consecrated abuses, made necessary in many nations by the weakness of the government, are secret accusations.[23] Their customary use makes men false and deceptive. Whoever can suspect another of being an informer beholds in him an enemy. Men then grow accustomed to masking their

22 [Cf. Montesquieu, *Spirit of the Laws*, XII, 12: "When considered by themselves, ⟨words⟩ have generally no determinate signification; for this depends on the time in which they are uttered. It often happens that in repeating the same words they have not the same meaning; this depends on their connection with other things, and sometimes more is signified by silence than by any expression whatever."]

23 [This chapter was directed particularly against the practice of the "state inquisitors" of the Venetian Republic. Montesquieu had noted that the Venetian practice was the consequence of the fact that the three powers of government—legislative, executive, and judiciary—were there exercised by the same body. Nevertheless, contrary to Beccaria, Montesquieu held that the Venetians of his day had "a very wise government." They had need, he held, of a secret magistracy to prevent ambitious noblemen from violating the law against acquisition of exorbitant wealth, and from setting plots "in secrecy and silence" to overthrow the established constitution. That is why, Montesquieu concludes, "a mouth of stone ⟨bocca del leone⟩ is open to every informer at Venice"; by using informers, the Venetian state inquisitors "restore, as it were by violence, the state to its liberty" (*Spirit*, II, 3; V, 8; IX, 6).]

true feelings and, used to hiding them from others, they finally arrive at concealing them from themselves. When men have arrived at that point, they are unhappy indeed! Lacking clear and fixed principles to guide them, they wander aimlessly, tossed about in the vast sea of opinions; ever busy trying to escape from the phantasms that menace them, they live through the present always embittered by the uncertainty of the future. Deprived of the lasting pleasures of peace and security, they devour in haste the few fleeting moments of such pleasure scattered through their wretched lives, as the sole consolation for their having lived. Of such men are we to make intrepid soldiers, defenders of country and throne? Are we to find, among these, incorruptible magistrates who, with a free and patriotic eloquence, will sustain and advance the true interests of the sovereign, and who, with their tributes, will carry to the throne the love and blessings of all classes of men, thereby bestowing, on palaces and cottages alike, not only peace and security, but also that zealous hope of ameliorating their lot, which is a most useful ferment and vital principle of states?

Who can defend himself against calumny when it comes armed with tyranny's strongest shield, *secrecy?* What strange sort of constitution must it be in which the ruler suspects every subject of being an enemy, and finds himself compelled, for the sake of public tranquility, to deprive each man of his personal share in it?

What are the arguments alleged in justification of secret accusations and punishments? The public welfare, the security and preservation of the form of government? But how strange a constitution is that wherein the wielder of force and public opinion, which is even more efficacious, is fearful of every citizen! The indemnity of the accuser? The laws, then, do not sufficiently protect him; and the conclusion must be that there are subjects more powerful than the sovereign! The infamy attached to the informer? In other words, secret calumnies are to be authorized and public ones punished! The nature of the crime? If indifferent actions, if even actions advantageous to the public, are called crimes, accusations and trials are never secret enough. Can there conceivably be crimes, that is, offenses committed against the public, of which the general interest does not require that a public example be made in an open trial? I respect all governments, and I speak of no one in particular. Circumstances may be such, sometimes, that when an evil is inherent in a national system an attempt to remove it may seem to precipitate utter ruin. But, were I called upon to dictate new laws in some abandoned corner of the universe, before authorizing such a practice, my hand would tremble and posterity would loom up before me.

Montesquieu has said that public accusations are more suited to a republic, in which the principal passion of citizens ought to be for the public good, than to a monarchy, where that feeling is extremely weak owing to the very nature of the government, and where the best practice is to assign commissioners who, in the name of the people, accuse the infractors of the laws. But every government, republican as well as monarchic, ought to inflict upon the false accuser the very punishment that the accused is supposed to receive.

X

SUGGESTIVE INTERROGATIONS. DEPOSITIONS

Our laws forbid the use of leading or *suggestive* questions in a trial, questions, that is, which, as the learned say, explore what is *special* in the circumstances of a crime, when they ought to be exploring what is *general*—those questions, in other words, which, because they have an immediate connection with the crime, *suggest* to the accused an immediate response. According to the criminologists, interrogations should, one might say, envelop a fact spirally, but never approach it by a straight line. The reasons for this procedure are either so as not to suggest to the accused an answer that confronts him with the accusation or, perhaps, because it seems to run against the very nature for an accused person to accuse himself directly. Whether it be one or the other of these two reasons, remarkable indeed is the contradiction in the laws which couple with this usage the authorization of torture. What possible interrogation can be more *suggestive* than pain? The first reason is surely applicable in the case of torture, for pain will *suggest* obstinate silence to a strong man, enabling him thereby to exchange a greater for a lesser punishment, and to the weak it will *suggest* confession, so that he may free himself from present torment which is, for the moment at least, more efficacious than the fear of future pain. The second reason is also evidently relevant here, for, if a *special* interrogation makes an accused person confess against his natural right, spasms of torture will do so the more easily. But men are ruled much more by the difference in the names of things than by the things themselves.

Finally, a person who, under examination, obstinately refuses to answer the questions asked of him deserves a punishment that should be fixed by law, and of the severest kind, so that men may not thus fail to provide the necessary example which they owe to the public. This punishment is not necessary when the guilt of the accused is beyond doubt. For in that case interrogations are useless in the same way that a confession of the crime is useless when other proofs are enough to establish guilt. This last case is the commonest, for experience shows that in most trials the accused deny their guilt.

XI

OATHS

Laws and the natural sentiments of man contradict one another when oaths are administered to the accused, binding him to be truthful when he can best serve his own interests by being false; as if a man could really swear to contribute to his own destruction; as if religion were not silent in most men when interest speaks. The experience of all ages has shown that men have abused this precious gift of heaven more than any other. And why should the wicked respect it when those who are esteemed the wisest of men have often violated it? For the majority of men, the motives which religion opposes to the tumult of fear and to love of life are too weak because they are too distant from the senses. The affairs of heaven are regulated by laws altogether different from those that regulate human affairs. Why compromise one with the other? Why confront a man with the terrible alternative of either sinning against God or concurring in his own ruin? The law that requires such an oath commands one to be either a bad Christian or a martyr. Little by little the oath is reduced to a mere formality, and the whole force of religious feelings, which for most men are the sole pledge of honesty, is destroyed. Experience has shown how useless oaths are. Every judge can be my witness that no oath ever made any criminal tell the truth. And reason is equally a witness, for it declares that all laws are useless, and consequently injurious, when they oppose the natural feelings of man. The fate of such laws is the same as that of dikes set up directly against the course of a river: either they break down immediately and are overrun or a whirlpool which they themselves form corrodes and undermines them imperceptibly.

XII

TORTURE [24]

A cruelty consecrated by the practice of most nations is torture of the accused during his trial, either to make him confess the crime or to clear up contradictory statements, or to discover accomplices, or to purge him of infamy in some metaphysical and incomprehensible way, or, finally, to discover other crimes of which he might be guilty but of which he is not accused.

No man can be called *guilty* before a judge has sentenced him, nor can society deprive him of public protection before it has been decided that he has in fact violated the conditions under which such protection was accorded him. What right is it, then, if not simply that of might, which empowers a judge to inflict punishment on a citizen while doubt still remains as to his guilt or innocence? Here is the dilemma, which is nothing new: the fact of the crime is either certain or uncertain; if certain, all that is due is the punishment established by the laws, and tortures are useless because the criminal's confession is useless; if uncertain, then one must not torture the innocent, for such, according to the laws, is a man whose crimes are not yet proved.

What is the political intent of punishments? To instill fear in other men. But what justification can we find, then, for the secret and private tortures which the tyranny of custom practices on the guilty and the innocent? It is important, indeed, to let no known crime pass unpunished, but it is useless to re-

[24] [The historical references and juridical citations of this celebrated chapter were supplied by Pietro Verri, who had, at the time this work was being written, already compiled his notes for the posthumously published *Osservazioni sulla tortura* (1804). Alessandro Manzoni, Beccaria's grandson, subjecting many of the citations to a very rigorous examination in his *Storia della Colonna Infame*, Chapter Two, has demonstrated that they are, for the most part, misrepresented in the accounts given by Verri and echoed by Beccaria. See Introduction, p. xxii.]

veal the author of a crime that lies deeply buried in darkness. A wrong already committed, and for which there is no remedy, ought to be punished by political society only because it might otherwise excite false hopes of impunity in others. If it be true that a greater number of men, whether because of fear or virtue, respect the laws than break them, then the risk of torturing an innocent person should be considered greater when, other things being equal, the probability is greater that a man has rather respected the laws than despised them.

But I say more: it tends to confound all relations to require that a man be at the same time accuser and accused, that pain be made the crucible of truth, as if its criterion lay in the muscles and sinews of a miserable wretch.

The law that authorizes torture is a law that says: "Men, resist pain; and if nature has created in you an inextinguishable self-love, if it has granted you an inalienable right of self-defense, I create in you an altogether contrary sentiment: a heroic hatred of yourselves; and I command you to accuse yourselves, to speak the truth even while muscles are being lacerated and bones disjointed."

This infamous crucible of truth is a still-standing memorial of the ancient and barbarous legislation of a time when trials by fire and by boiling water, as well as the uncertain outcomes of duels, were called "judgments of God," [25] as if the links of

25 [Beccaria, following Verri, is quite mistaken in asserting that torture is of the same juridical order as "trials by fire or boiling water." On the contrary, when men trust the competence of gods, or of a jury of their fellow men, to determine guilt or innocence, the confession which torture is meant to extract from the accused becomes superfluous. It is only when men lose their trust in gods or in human jurors that the law must search for a witness of greater authority. Historically it is possible to demonstrate that torture of the accused has sometimes been introduced simply as a desperate abuse of the rationalistic desire to secure that "consent of the governed" which alone "justifies" governmental power, even when the power to be exercised is that of criminal punishment. For a brief summary of the relations between appeals to God, proofs by oaths, proofs by ordeals, judicial combats, indictments by jury, trial by jury, and torture, in the development of Anglo-American legal procedures, see *The Col-*

the eternal chain, which is in the bosom of the First Cause, must at every moment be disordered and broken by frivolous human arrangements. The only difference between torture and trials by fire and boiling water is that the outcome seems to depend, in the first, on the will of the accused, and in the second, on a purely physical and extrinsic fact; but this difference is only apparent, not real. One is as much free to tell the truth in the midst of convulsions and torments, as one was free then to impede without fraud the effects of fire and boiling water. Every act of our will is invariably proportioned to the force of the sensory impression which is its source; and the sensory capacity of every man is limited. Thus the impression of pain may become so great that, filling the entire sensory capacity of the tortured person, it leaves him free only to choose what for the moment is the shortest way of escape from pain. The response of the accused is then as inevitable as the impressions of fire and water. The sensitive innocent man will then confess himself guilty when he believes that, by so doing, he can put an end to his torment. Every difference between guilt and innocence disappears by virtue of the very means one pretends to be using to discover it. [Torture] is an infallible means indeed—for absolving robust scoundrels and for condemning innocent persons who happen to be weak. Such are the fatal defects of this so-called criterion of truth, a criterion fit for a cannibal, which the Romans, who were barbarous themselves on many counts, reserved only for slaves, the victims of a fierce and overly praised virtue.[26]

Of two men, equally innocent or equally guilty, the strong and courageous will be acquitted, the weak and timid condemned, by virtue of this rigorous rational argument: "I, the

---

lected Papers of Frederic William Maitland, ed. H. A. L. Fisher (Cambridge, 1911), II, 445-65.]

[26] [It has been noted that Roman jurists, as well as Roman philosophers, including Cicero, Seneca, Quintilian, and Ulpian, had written eloquently against the abuse and often even against the use of torture in juridical proceedings. Verri cites a number of their views in his Osservazioni, but minimizes their significance. Cf. St. Augustine, The City of God, XIX, 6.]

judge, was supposed to find you guilty of such and such a crime; you, the strong, have been able to resist the pain, and I therefore absolve you; you, the weak, have yielded, and I therefore condemn you. I am aware that a confession wrenched forth by torments ought to be of no weight whatsoever, but I'll torment you again if you don't confirm what you have confessed."

The effect of torture, therefore, is a matter of temperament and calculation that varies with each man according to his strength and sensibility, so that, with this method, a mathematician could more readily than a judge resolve this problem: given the muscular force and nervous sensibility of an innocent person, find the degree of pain that will make him confess himself guilty of a given crime.

The examination of an accused person is undertaken to ascertain the truth. But if this truth is difficult to discover in the air, gesture, and countenance of a man at ease, much more difficult will its discovery be when the convulsions of pain have distorted all the signs by which truth reveals itself in spite of themselves in the countenances of the majority of men. Every violent action confounds and dissolves those little differences in objects by means of which one may occasionally distinguish the true from the false.

A strange consequence that necessarily follows from the use of torture is that the innocent person is placed in a condition worse than that of the guilty, for if both are tortured, the circumstances are all against the former. Either he confesses the crime and is condemned, or he is declared innocent and has suffered a punishment he did not deserve. The guilty man, on the contrary, finds himself in a favorable situation; that is, if, as a consequence of having firmly resisted the torture, he is absolved as innocent, he will have escaped a greater punishment by enduring a lesser one. Thus the innocent cannot but lose, whereas the guilty may gain.

This truth is felt, finally though confusedly, by those very persons who shrink furthest from it in practice. The confession made under torture is of no avail if it be not confirmed with an oath after the torture has stopped, but if the accused does not then confirm the crime, he is again tortured. Some jurists, and some nations, allow this infamous begging of principles to be repeated no more than three times; other nations, and other jurists, leave it to the discretion of the judge. It would be superfluous to intensify the light, here, by citing the innumerable examples of innocent persons who have confessed themselves criminals because of the agonies of torture; there is no nation, there is no age that does not have its own to cite; but neither will men change nor will they deduce the necessary consequences. Every man who has ever extended his thought even a little beyond the mere necessities of life has at least sometimes felt an urge to run toward Nature, who, with secret and indistinct voices, calls him to her; custom, that tyrant of minds, drives him back and frightens him.

Torture is alleged to be useful, also, as applied to suspected criminals, when they contradict themselves under examination; as if fear of punishment, the uncertainty of the sentence, the pomp and majesty of the judge, the almost universal ignorance of both the wicked and the innocent, were not apt enough to plunge the innocent man who is afraid, as well as the guilty who is seeking to conceal, into contradiction; as if contradictions, which are common enough in men when they are at ease, are not likely to be multiplied in the perturbations of a mind altogether absorbed in the thought of saving itself from imminent peril.

Torture is applied to discover whether the criminal is guilty of crimes other than those of which he is accused; it amounts to this sort of reasoning: "You are guilty of one crime, therefore it is possible that you are guilty also of a hundred others; this doubt weighs on me, and I want to convince myself one way or another by using my criterion of truth: the laws torture you because you are guilty, because you may be guilty, because I insist that you be guilty."

Torture is applied to an accused person to discover his accomplices in the crime. But if it is demonstrated that torture is not an opportune means for discovering the truth, how can it serve to reveal the accomplices, which is one of the truths to be discovered? As if a man who accuses himself would not more readily accuse others. Is it right to torment men for the crime of another? Will not the accomplices be disclosed from the examination of witnesses, from the examination of the accused, from the proofs and from the material fact of the crime—in sum, from all of the very means that should serve to convict the accused of having committed the crime? Accomplices usually fly as soon as their companion is taken; the uncertainty of their lot of itself condemns them to exile, and frees the nation from the danger of further offenses, while the punishment of the criminal who is taken achieves its sole purpose, which is to deter other men, by fear, from committing a similar crime.

Another ridiculous pretext for torture is purgation from infamy; which is to say, a man judged infamous by the laws must confirm his deposition with the dislocation of his bones. This abuse should not be tolerated in the eighteenth century. It is believed that pain, which is a sensation, can purge infamy, which is a purely moral relationship. Is torture perhaps a crucible, and infamy, perhaps, a mixed impure substance? But infamy is a sentiment subject neither to the laws nor to reason, but to common opinion. Torture itself brings real infamy to its victims. Thus, by this method, infamy is to be removed by adding to it.

It is not difficult to trace the origin of this ridiculous law, because the very absurdities that are adopted by an entire nation have always some relation to other common ideas that it respects. The usage seems to have derived from religious and spiritual ideas, which exert a great influence on the thoughts of men, nations, and ages. An infallible dogma assures us that the stains contracted through our human frailty, which have not merited the eternal anger of the Grand Being, must be purged by an incomprehensible fire. Now infamy is a civil stain, and as suffering and fire remove spiritual and incorporeal stains, why should not spasms of torture remove the civil stain, which is infamy? I believe that the confession of the criminal which is exacted as essential for condemnation in certain tribunals has a similar origin, for in the mysterious tribunal of penance the confession of sins is an essential part of the sacrament. Thus do men abuse the surest lights of Revelation, and as these are the only ones that subsist in times of ignorance, docile humanity turns to them on all occasions and makes of them the most absurd and far-fetched applications.

These truths were known to the Roman legislators, among whom one does not encounter the use of torture, except with slaves, who were denied any personality. They are adopted by England, a nation whose glorious attainments in literature, whose superiority in commerce and in wealth, and consequently in power, and whose examples of virtue and of courage, leave no doubt as to the goodness of her laws. Torture has been abolished in Sweden: abolished by one of the wisest monarchs of Europe,[27] who, having brought philosophy to the throne, a legislator that befriends subjects, has rendered them equal and free in dependence on the laws; this is the sole equality and liberty that reasonable men can desire in the present state of things. Torture is not deemed necessary in the laws that regulate armies, though these are, for the most part, made up of the dregs of nations, which would seem to have more use for it than any other class. How strange a thing, indeed, it must seem to anyone who fails to consider how great is the tyranny of usage that the laws of peace should have to learn a more humane method of judgment from spirits hardened to slaughter and bloodshed!

[27] [The punctuation suggests that Beccaria is writing of the king responsible for the abolition of torture in Sweden referred to in the first part of the sentence. However, Gustavus III (1746-1792), an enlightened monarch to whom Beccaria's words might well apply, did not attain the throne until 1771, seven years after Beccaria's treatise was published. The reference is perhaps to Frederick II of Prussia (1712-1786).]

XIII

PROSECUTIONS AND PRESCRIPTIONS [28]

After proofs of a crime have been introduced and its certainty determined, the criminal must be allowed opportune time and means for his defense—but time so brief as not to interfere with that promptness of punishment which we have seen to be one of the principal checks against crime. A mistaken love of humanity seems opposed to this brevity of time, but all doubt will vanish if one considers that the dangers to which innocence is exposed increase in proportion to the defectiveness of legislation.

But the laws should fix a definite length of time both for the defense of the accused and for the proof of crimes; the judge would become a legislator were he to decide the time necessary for the latter. Likewise, those atrocious crimes which are long remembered do not, when they have been proved, merit any prescription in favor of the criminal who has spared himself by flight; but in the case of minor and hidden crimes there should be a prescription relieving the citizen of uncertainty as to his lot, for the long obscurity in which his crimes have been involved removes the example of impunity, and the possibility remains, meanwhile, for the criminal to make amends. I merely indicate the principles, for a precise limitation can be fixed only for a given system of legislation and in the given circumstances of a society. I shall only add that, the advantage of moderate punishments in a nation having been demonstrated, the laws that shorten or extend the time of prescription or the time for proof according to the gravity of the crimes—thus making imprisonment itself, or voluntary exile, a part of the punishment—will provide an easy classification made up of few punishments, most of them mild, for a great number of crimes.

[28] [As used by Beccaria, the term "prescription" (*prescrizione*) must be understood to mean "limitation of criminal prosecution."]

But these time limits should not increase exactly in proportion to the atrocity of the crimes, since the probability of crimes is in inverse proportion to their atrocity. The time for inquiry should be shortened accordingly, and that of prescription increased, which would seem to contradict what I said before, namely, that equal punishments may be decreed for unequal crimes by counting as punishment the time of detention or of prescription which precedes the sentence. To clarify my idea for the reader, I distinguish two classes of crimes: the first is that of atrocious crimes, and this begins with homicide and includes all graver offenses; the second is that of minor crimes. This distinction is founded on human nature. The security of one's own life is a natural right; the security of one's property is a social right. The motives that induce men to transgress their natural feeling of compassion are fewer in number than those which, because of a natural desire to be happy, induce them to violate a right which they do not find registered in their hearts, but only in the conventions of society. The considerable difference of probability in each of these two classes of crimes requires that they be governed by diverse principles. In the more atrocious crimes, which are the least common, the time for inquiry should be decreased because of the increased probability that the accused may be innocent; the time of prescription should be increased, because only a definitive sentence of innocence or guilt can remove the illusory prospect of impunity, the harm of which increases with the atrocity of the crime. But in minor cases, since the probability of innocence of the accused is less, the time of inquiry should be extended, and since the harm of impunity is less, the time of prescription should also be shorter. Needless to say such a division of crimes into two classes could not be admitted were danger of impunity to decrease as much as the probability of the crimes increases. It is to be remembered that an accused person whose innocence or guilt is not established, free though he may be for want of proof, can be subjected to new imprisonment and to new inquiry for the same crime if fresh evidences prescribed by the law are intro-

duced, so long as the time of prescription fixed for his crime
has not passed. This, at any rate, seems to me to be the ar-
rangement best suited for protecting both the security and the
liberty of subjects, either of which is too likely to be favored
at the expense of the other; and thus these two blessings that
form the inalienable and equal patrimony of every citizen will
be left unprotected and uncared for, the one against open or
concealed despotism, the other against turbulent popular anarchy.

There are some crimes that are at the same time frequent in
society and difficult to prove. In these the difficulty of proof
is a measure of the probability of innocence; the harm of impunity being of less account, as the frequency of these crimes
depends on principles other than the dangers of impunity, the
time for inquiry and that of prescription should be equally
diminished. Yet adultery and pederasty, which are crimes difficult to prove, are precisely those which, according to the accepted principles, admit of tyrannical presumptions, of *quasi-
proofs,* and *semi-proofs,* as if a man could be semi-innocent
or semi-guilty, that is, semi-punishable or semi-absolvable;
[these are crimes in which] torture exercises its cruel power
on the person of the accused, on the witnesses, and even on
the whole family of the unfortunate wretch, as is taught with
icy brutality by certain sages who are supposed to serve as
the norm and law for judges.

In view of these principles, it will seem strange, to any one
who has not reflected that reason has almost never been the
legislator of nations, that the most atrocious or the most obscure or chimerical of crimes, that is, the least probable, are
established by conjectures and by the weakest and most equivocal proofs, as if the laws and the judge were primarily interested not in inquiry after the truth but in proving the crime
—as if the risk of condemning an innocent person were not
so much the greater as the probability of innocence surpasses
that of guilt.

Most men lack the vigor which is as much necessary for
great crimes as for great virtues; thus it seems that the two

always tend to occur simultaneously in those nations that support themselves by strenuous activity of government and of
the passions that conspire to the public good rather than by
their size or the constant goodness of the laws. In these, the
weakened passions seem more adapted to maintain than to im-
prove the form of government. From this an important consequence may be drawn, namely, that great crimes in a nation
are not always a proof of its decadence.

XIV

ATTEMPTS, ACCOMPLICES, IMPUNITY

Laws do not punish intent; but surely an act undertaken
with the manifest intention of committing a crime deserves
punishment, though less than that which is due upon the
actual execution of the crime. The importance of preventing
a criminal attempt authorizes punishment, but as there may
be an interval between the attempt and the execution, reser-
vation of greater punishment for the accomplished crime may
lead to repentance. The same applies, but for a different reason, when there are several accomplices of a crime, not all of
them involved as its immediate perpetrators. When a number
of men join in taking a risk, the greater it is, the more do they
endeavor to equalize it for all. It will be more difficult, then,
to find anyone actually willing to execute the crime, involving
him in a greater risk than the others. The only exception
would be where a special reward were fixed for the executor,
for in that case, since he is compensated for the greater risk,
the punishment ought to be equal. Such reflections may seem
philosophically too refined for those who fail to consider how
important it is that the laws should leave the least possible
grounds for accord among companions in crime.

Some tribunals offer impunity to the accomplice in a great
crime who will reveal his companions. Such an expedient has

disadvantages as well as advantages. The disadvantages are that the nation authorizes treachery, which even scoundrels detest in themselves, and also, that crimes of courage are less fatal to a nation than those of cowardice. The first sort is not of frequent occurrence and merely awaits a beneficent, directive force to make it conspire to the public good, while cowardice is more common and contagious and always the more self-concentrating. Besides, the tribunal simply reveals its own uncertainty and the weakness of its law when it has to implore the aid of an offender. The advantages [of offering impunity] are the prevention of great crimes which intimidate the populace because their effects are revealed while their authors remain hidden; the practice helps, moreover, to show that a person who breaks faith with the laws, that is, with the public, will probably break faith also in private. It would seem to me that a general law promising impunity to the accomplice who reveals a crime would be preferable to a special declaration in a particular case, for the mutual fear that each accomplice would then have of being alone in his risk would prevent associations; the tribunal would not, then, encourage the audacity of criminals by allowing them to feel that in a particular case their aid was required. Such a law, however, should accompany impunity with banishment of the informer. . . . But I torment myself uselessly trying to overcome the remorse I feel in authorizing the inviolable laws, the monument of public trust, the basis of human morality, to countenance treachery and dissimulation. What example would it be to the nation, then, if the promised impunity were not accorded, if, by means of learned cavils, the person accepting the law's invitation were dragged to punishment, in spite of the public trust? Such examples are not rare among nations, and far from rare, therefore, are those who have no other idea of a nation than of a complicated mechanism whose parts the cleverest and strongest move according to their talents. Cold, and insensible to all that forms the delight of tender and lofty spirits, with imperturbable sagacity they excite the tenderest feelings and the most violent passions whenever they deem them useful to their ends, playing on men's hearts like musicians on instruments.

VX

MILDNESS OF PUNISHMENTS

From simple consideration of the truths thus far presented it is evident that the purpose of punishment is neither to torment and afflict a sensitive being, nor to undo a crime already committed. Can there, in a body politic which, far from acting on passion, is the tranquil moderator of private passions—can there be a place for this useless cruelty, for this instrument of wrath and fanaticism, or of weak tyrants? Can the shrieks of a wretch recall from time, which never reverses its course, deeds already accomplished? The purpose can only be to prevent the criminal from inflicting new injuries on its citizens and to deter others from similar acts.[29] Always keeping due proportions, such punishments and such method of inflicting them ought to be chosen, therefore, which will make the strongest and most lasting impression on the minds of men, and inflict the least torment on the body of the criminal.

Who, in reading history, can keep from cringing with horror before the spectacle of barbarous and useless torments, cold-bloodedly devised and carried through by men who called themselves wise? What man of any sensibility can keep from shuddering when he sees thousands of poor wretches driven by a misery either intended or tolerated by the laws (which have always favored the few and outraged the many) to a desperate return to the original state of nature—when he sees them accused of impossible crimes, fabricated by timid ignorance, or found guilty of nothing other than being true to their own

[29] [Cf. Seneca, *De Clementia* I, 16: "No man punishes because a sin has been committed, but that sin may not be committed. For what has passed cannot be recalled, but what is to come may be prevented."]

principles, and sees them lacerated with meditated formality and slow torture by men gifted with the same senses, and consequently with the same passions? Happy spectacle for a fanatical multitude!

For a punishment to attain its end, the evil which it inflicts has only to exceed the advantage derivable from the crime; in this excess of evil one should include the certainty of punishment and the loss of the good which the crime might have produced.[30] All beyond this is superfluous and for that reason tyrannical. Men are regulated in their conduct by the repeated impression of evils they know, and not according to those of which they are ignorant. Given, for example, two nations, in one of which, in the scale of punishments proportioned to the scale of crimes, the maximum punishment is perpetual slavery, and in the other the wheel; I say that the first shall have as much fear of its maximum punishment as the second; whatever reason might be adduced for introducing to the first the maximum punishment of the other could similarly be adduced to justify intensification of punishments in the latter, passing imperceptibly from the wheel to slower and more ingenious torments, and at length to the ultimate refinements of a science only too well known to tyrants.

In proportion as torments become more cruel, the spirits of men, which are like fluids that always rise to the level of surrounding objects, become callous, and the ever lively force of the passions brings it to pass that after a hundred years of cruel torments the wheel inspires no greater fear than imprisonment once did. The severity of punishment of itself emboldens men to commit the very wrongs it is supposed to prevent; they are driven to commit additional crimes to avoid the punishment for a single one. The countries and times most notorious for severity of penalties have always been those in

30 [Considering the law of the "state of nature," Locke writes (Second Treatise, II, 12): "Each transgression may be punished to that degree and with so much severity as will suffice to make it an ill bargain to the offender, give him cause to repent, and terrify others from doing the like" (Library of Liberal Arts edn., No. 31 [New York, 1952], p. 9).]

which the bloodiest and most inhumane of deeds were committed, for the same spirit of ferocity that guided the hand of the legislators also ruled that of the parricide and assassin. On the throne it dictated iron laws for vicious-spirited slaves to obey, while in private, hiddenly, it instigated the slaughter of tyrants only to make room for new ones.

Two other baneful consequences derive from the cruelty of punishments, interfering with the avowed purpose of preventing crimes. The first is that it is not easy to establish a proper proportion between crime and punishment because, however much an industrious cruelty may have multiplied the variety of its forms, they cannot exceed in force the limits of endurance determined by human organization and sensibility. When once those limits are reached, it is impossible to devise, for still more injurious and atrocious crimes, any additional punishment that could conceivably serve to prevent them. The other consequence is that impunity itself results from the atrocity of penalties. Men are bound within limits, no less in evil than in good; a spectacle too atrocious for humanity can only be a passing rage, never a permanent system such as the laws must be, for if [the laws] are really cruel, they must either be changed or fatal impunity will follow from the laws themselves.

I conclude with this reflection that the scale of punishments should be relative to the state of the nation itself. Very strong and sensible impressions are demanded for the callous spirits of a people that has just emerged from the savage state. A lightning bolt is necessary to stop a ferocious lion that turns upon the shot of a rifle. But to the extent that spirits are softened in the social state, sensibility increases and, as it increases, the force of punishment must diminish if the relation between object and sensory impression is to be kept constant.[31]

[31] [Cf. Montesquieu, *Spirit*, VI, 12: "Experience shows that in countries remarkable for the lenity of their laws the spirit of the inhabitants is as much affected by slight penalties as in other countries by severer punishments."]

XVI

THE DEATH PENALTY

This useless prodigality of torments, which has never made men better, has prompted me to examine whether death is really useful and just in a well-organized government.[32]

What manner of right can men attribute to themselves to slaughter their fellow beings? Certainly not that from which sovereignty and the laws derive. These are nothing but the sum of the least portions of the private liberty of each person; they represent the general will, which is the aggregate of particular wills. Was there ever a man who can have wished to leave to other men the choice of killing him? Is it conceivable that the least sacrifice of each person's liberty should include sacrifice of the greatest of all goods, life? And if that were the case, how could such a principle be reconciled with the other, that man is not entitled to take his own life? He must be, if he can surrender that right to others or to society as a whole.

The punishment of death, therefore, is not a right, for I have demonstrated that it cannot be such; but it is the war of a nation against a citizen whose destruction it judges to be necessary or useful. If, then, I can show that death is neither useful nor necessary I shall have gained the cause of humanity.

32 [An argument similar to that of this famous chapter was advanced, according to Thucydides (III, 45), in the Athenian debate (427 B.C.) over the punishment to be accorded the citizens of rebellious Mytilene. Diodotus, the opponent of severity, said: "Men have gone through the whole catalog of penalties in the hope that, by increasing their severity, they may suffer less at the hands of evildoers. In early ages the punishments, even of the worst offenses, would naturally be milder; but as time went on and mankind continued to transgress, they seldom stopped short of death. And still there were transgressors. Some greater terror then had yet to be discovered; certainly death is no deterrent." But Diodotus, unlike Beccaria, concludes with a repudiation of the very idea of deterrence as justification for punishment: "In a word then, it is impossible and simply absurd to suppose that human nature when bent upon some favorite project can be restrained either by the strength of law or by any other terror."]

46 BECCARIA

There are only two possible motives for believing that the death of a citizen is necessary. The first: when it is evident that even if deprived of liberty he still has connections and power such as endanger the security of the nation—when, that is, his existence can produce a dangerous revolution in the established form of government. The death of a citizen thus becomes necessary when a nation is recovering or losing its liberty or, in time of anarchy, when disorders themselves take the place of laws. But while the laws reign tranquilly, in a form of government enjoying the consent of the entire nation, well defended externally and internally by force, and by opinion, which is perhaps even more efficacious than force, where executive power is lodged with the true sovereign alone, where riches purchase pleasures and not authority, I see no necessity for destroying a citizen, except if his death were the only real way of restraining others from committing crimes; this is the second motive for believing that the death penalty may be just and necessary.

If the experience of all the ages, in which the supreme penalty has never prevented determined men from injuring society, if the example of the Roman citizenry,[33] and twenty years of the reign of Elizabeth of Moscow,[34] in which she gave to the fathers of the people an illustrious example worth at least as much as many conquests purchased with the blood of children of the fatherland—if all this should fail to persuade men to whom the language of reason is always suspect, and that of authority always efficacious, it suffices merely to consult human nature to perceive the truth of my assertion.

It is not the intensity of punishment that has the greatest

[33] [Cf. Sir Henry Sumner Maine, *Ancient Law* (Oxford, 1946), pp. 322-24. Maine asserts that the "disappearance of the punishment of Death from the penal system of Republican Rome . . . led distinctly and directly to those frightful Revolutionary intervals, known as the Proscriptions, during which all law was formally suspended simply because party violence could find no other avenue to the vengeance for which it was thirsting."]

[34] [During the reign (1741-1762) of the Empress Elizabeth, capital punishment was not practiced in Russia.]

effect on the human spirit, but its duration, for our sensibility is more easily and more permanently affected by slight but repeated impressions than by a powerful but momentary action. The sway of habit is universal over every sentient being; as man speaks and walks and satisfies his needs by its aid, so the ideas of morality come to be stamped upon the mind only by long and repeated impressions. It is not the terrible yet momentary spectacle of the death of a wretch, but the long and painful example of a man deprived of liberty, who, having become a beast of burden, recompenses with his labors the society he has offended, which is the strongest curb against crimes. That efficacious idea—efficacious, because very often repeated to ourselves—"I myself shall be reduced to so long and miserable a condition if I commit a similar misdeed" is far more potent than the idea of death, which men envision always at an obscure distance.

The death penalty leaves an impression which, with all its force, cannot make up for the tendency to forget, natural to man even with regard to the most essential things, and readily accelerated by the passions. A general rule: violent passions surprise men, but not for long, and are therefore apt to bring on those revolutions which instantly transform ordinary men either into Persians or Lacedemonians; but in a free and peaceful government the impressions should be frequent rather than strong.

The death penalty becomes for the majority a spectacle and for some others an object of compassion mixed with disdain; these two sentiments rather than the salutary fear which the laws pretend to inspire occupy the spirits of the spectators. But in moderate and prolonged punishments the dominant sentiment is the latter, because it is the only one. The limit which the legislator ought to fix on the rigor of punishments would seem to be determined by the sentiment of compassion itself, when it begins to prevail over every other in the hearts of those who are the witnesses of punishment, inflicted for their sake rather than for the criminal's.

For a punishment to be just it should consist of only such

gradations of intensity as suffice to deter men from committing crimes. Now, the person does not exist who, reflecting upon it, could choose for himself total and perpetual loss of personal liberty, no matter how advantageous a crime might seem to be. Thus the intensity of the punishment of a life sentence of servitude, in place of the death penalty, has in it what suffices to deter any determined spirit. It has, let me add, even more. Many men are able to look calmly and with firmness upon death—some from fanaticism, some from vanity, which almost always accompanies man even beyond the tomb, some from a final and desperate attempt either to live no longer or to escape their misery. But neither fanaticism nor vanity can subsist among fetters or chains, under the rod, under the yoke, in a cage of iron, where the desperate wretch does not end his woes but merely begins them. Our spirit resists violence and extreme but momentary pains more easily than it does time and incessant weariness, for it can, so to speak, collect itself for a moment to repel the first, but the vigor of its elasticity does not suffice to resist the long and repeated action of the second.

With the death penalty, every example given to the nation presupposes a new crime; with the penalty of a lifetime of servitude a single crime supplies frequent and lasting examples. And if it be important that men frequently observe the power of the laws, penal executions ought not to be separated by long intervals; they, therefore, presuppose frequency of the crimes. Thus, if this punishment is to be really useful, it somehow must not make the impression on men that it should; that is, it must be useful and not useful at the same time. To anyone raising the argument that perpetual servitude is as painful as death and therefore equally cruel, I will reply that, adding up all the moments of unhappiness of servitude, it may well be even more cruel; but these are drawn out over an entire lifetime, while the pain of death exerts its whole force in a moment. And precisely this is the advantage of penal servitude, that it inspires terror in the spectator more than in the sufferer, for the former considers the entire sum of unhappy moments, while the latter is distracted from the thought of future misery by that of the present moment. All evils are magnified in the imagination, and the sufferer finds compensations and consolations unknown and incredible to spectators who substitute their own sensibility for the callous spirit of a miserable wretch.

This, more or less, is the line of reasoning of a thief or an assassin—men who find no motive weighty enough to keep them from violating the laws, except the gallows or the wheel. I know that cultivation of the sentiments of one's own spirit is an art that is learned through education; but although a thief may not be able to give a clear account of his motives, that does not make them any the less operative: "What are these laws that I am supposed to respect, that place such a great distance between me and the rich man? He refuses me the penny I ask of him and, as an excuse, tells me to sweat at work that he knows nothing about. Who made these laws? Rich and powerful men who have never deigned to visit the squalid huts of the poor, who have never had to share a crust of moldy bread amid the innocent cries of hungry children and the tears of a wife. Let us break these bonds, fatal to the majority and only useful to a few indolent tyrants; let us attack the injustice at its source. I will return to my natural state of independence; I shall at least for a little time live free and happy with the fruits of my courage and industry. The day will perhaps come for my sorrow and repentance, but it will be brief, and for a single day of suffering I shall have many years of liberty and of pleasures. As king over a few, I will correct the mistakes of fortune and will see these tyrants grow pale and tremble in the presence of one whom with an insulting flourish of pride they used to dismiss to a lower level than their horses and dogs." Then religion presents itself to the mind of the abusive wretch and, promising him an easy repentance and an almost certain eternity of happiness, does much to diminish for him the horror of that ultimate tragedy.

But he who foresees a great number of years, or even a whole lifetime to be spent in servitude and pain, in sight of his fel-

low citizens with whom he lives in freedom and friendship,
slave of the laws which once afforded him protection, makes
a useful comparison of all this with the uncertainty of the result of his crimes, and the brevity of the time in which he
would enjoy their fruits. The perpetual example of those
whom he actually sees the victims of their own carelessness
makes a much stronger impression upon him than the spectacle
of a punishment that hardens more than it corrects him.

The death penalty cannot be useful, because of the example
of barbarity it gives men. If the passions or the necessities of
war have taught the shedding of human blood, the laws, mod-
erators of the conduct of men, should not extend the beastly
example, which becomes more pernicious since the inflicting
of legal death is attended with much study and formality. It
seems to me absurd that the laws, which are an expression of
the public will, which detest and punish homicide, should
themselves commit it, and that to deter citizens from murder,
they order a public one. Which are the true and most useful
laws? Those pacts and those conditions which all would observe and propose, while the voice of private interest, which
one cannot help hearing, is either silent or in accord with that
of the public. What are the sentiments of each and every man
about the death penalty? Let us read them in the acts of indignation and contempt with which everyone regards the hang-
man, who is, after all, merely the innocent executor of the
public will, a good citizen contributing to the public good, an
instrument as necessary to the internal security of a people as
valorous soldiers are to the external. What then is the origin
of this contradiction? And why, in spite of reason, is this sentiment indelible in men? Because men, in the most secret recess
of their spirits, in the part that more than any other still con-
serves the original form of their first nature, have always believed that one's own life can be in the power of no one, except necessity alone which, with its scepter of iron, rules the
universe.

What must men think when they see learned magistrates and
high ministers of justice, who, with calm indifference, cause a

criminal to be dragged, by slow proceedings, to death; and while some wretch quakes in the last throes of anguish, awaiting the fatal blow, the judge who, with insensitive coldness, and perhaps even with secret satisfaction in his personal authority, passes by to enjoy the conveniences and the pleasures of life? "Ah!" they will say, "these laws are but the pretexts of force; the studied and cruel formalities of justice are nothing but a conventional language for immolating us with greater security, like victims destined for sacrifice to the insatiable idol of despotism. Assassination, which is represented to us as a terrible misdeed, we see employed without any repugnance and without excitement. Let us take advantage of the example given us. Violent death seemed to be a terrible spectacle in their descriptions, but we see that it is the affair of a moment. How much less terrible must it be for one who, not expecting it, is spared almost all there is in it of pain!"

Such are the dangerous and fallacious arguments employed, if not with clarity, at least confusedly, by men disposed to crimes, in whom, as we have seen, the abuse of religion is more potent than religion itself.

If one were to cite against me the example of all the ages and of almost all the nations that have applied the death penalty to certain crimes, my reply would be that the example reduced itself to nothing in the face of truth, against which there is no prescription; that the history of men leaves us with the impression of a vast sea of errors, among which, at great intervals, some rare and hardly intelligible truths appear to float on the surface. Human sacrifices were once common to almost all nations, yet who will dare to defend them? That only a few societies, and for a short time only, have abstained from applying the death penalty, stands in my favor rather than against me, for that conforms with the usual lot of great truths, which are about as long-lasting as a lightning flash in comparison with the long dark night that envelops mankind. The happy time has not yet arrived in which truth shall be the portion of the greatest number, as error has heretofore been. And from this universal law those truths only have been exempted which Infinite Wisdom has chosen to distinguish from others by revealing them.

The voice of a philosopher is too weak to contend against the tumults and the cries of so many who are guided by blind custom, but the few wise men who are scattered over the face of the earth shall in their heart of hearts echo what I say; and if the truth, among the infinite obstacles that keep it from a monarch, in spite of himself, should ever reach as far as his throne, let him know that it comes there with the secret approval of all men; let him know that in his worthy presence the bloody fame of conquerors will be silenced, and that posterity, which is just, assigns him first place among the peaceful trophies of the Tituses, of the Antonines, and of the Trajans.[35]

How fortunate humanity would be if laws were for the first time being decreed for it, now that we see on the thrones of Europe monarchs who are beneficent, who encourage peaceful virtues, the sciences, the arts, who are fathers to their peoples, crowned citizens, the increase of whose authority constitutes the happiness of subjects, because it removes that intermediate despotism, the more cruel because less secure, which represses popular expressions of esteem which are ever sincere and ever of good omen when they can reach the throne! If these monarchs, I say, suffer the old laws to subsist, it is because of the infinite difficulties involved in stripping from errors the venerated rust of many centuries. This surely is a reason for enlightened citizens to desire, with greater ardor, the continual increase of their authority.

[35] [Titus Flavius Sabinus Vespasianus (A.D. 40?-81), Marcus Ulpius Trajanus (A.D. 52-117), and Antoninus Pius (A.D. 86-161) were all Roman emperors who were noted for their beneficence and concern for the welfare of their subjects.

Hegel writes (Philosophy of Right, p. 247): "Beccaria's endeavour to have capital punishment abolished has had beneficial effects. Even if neither Joseph II nor the French ever succeeded in entirely abolishing it, still we have begun to see which crimes deserve the death sentence and which do not. Capital punishment has thus become rarer, as in fact should be the case with this most extreme punishment."]

XVII

BANISHMENT AND CONFISCATIONS

Anyone who disturbs the public peace, who does not obey the laws, that is, the conditions under which men agree to support and defend one another, must be excluded from society —he must be banished from it.

It seems that banishment should be imposed on those who, being accused of an atrocious crime, have against them a great probability, but no certainty of guilt; but for this it is necessary to have a statute as little arbitrary and as precise as possible, which condemns to banishment whoever has forced upon the nation the fatal alternative either of fearing or of unjustly punishing him, leaving him, however, the sacred right to prove his innocence. The motives should, therefore, be stronger against a citizen than against a foreigner, against a person accused for the first time than against one who has often been accused.

But should a person banished and excluded forever from the society of which he was a member be deprived of his possessions? Such a question may be viewed in various aspects. The loss of possessions is a punishment greater than that of banishment; in some cases, therefore, according to the crimes, all or a part of one's possessions should be forfeited, and in others, none. Forfeiture of all should follow when the banishment prescribed by the law is such that it nullifies all ties between society and a delinquent citizen; in that case, the citizen dies and the man remains. With respect to the body politic, [civil death] should produce the same effect as natural death. It would seem, then, that the possessions of which the criminal is deprived should pass to his legitimate heirs rather than to the ruler, since death and such banishment are the same with regard to the body politic. But it is not on the grounds of this subtlety that I dare to disapprove of the confiscation of goods. If some have maintained that confiscations have served to re-

strain vengeful acts and abuses of personal power, they fail to
consider that, although punishments produce some good, they
are not always therefore just, for to be so they must be necessary; even a useful injustice cannot be tolerated by the legislator who means to close all doors against that watchful tyranny which entices with temporary advantages and with the
apparent happiness of a few illustrious persons, disdainful of
the ruin to come and the tears of multitudes in obscurity. Confiscations put a price on the heads of the weak, cause the innocent to suffer the punishment of the guilty, and force the
innocent themselves into the desperate necessity of committing crimes. What spectacle can be sadder than that of a
family dragged into infamy and misery by the crimes of its
head which the submission ordained by the laws would hinder
the family from preventing, even if it had the means to do so.

XVIII

INFAMY

Infamy is a mark of public disapprobation that deprives
the criminal of public esteem, of the confidence of his country, and of that almost fraternal intimacy which society inspires. It cannot be determined by law. The infamy which the
law inflicts, therefore, must be the same as that which arises
from the relations of things, the same that is dictated by universal morality, or by the particular morality of particular
systems, which are legislators of vulgar opinions and of that
particular nation. If one [set of opinions] differs from the
other, either the law suffers a loss of public respect or the ideas
of morality and probity vanish in spite of declamations that
can never withstand the weight of examples. Whoever declares
actions to be infamous that are in themselves indifferent diminishes the infamy of actions that are really such.

Corporal and painful punishments should not be applied
to crimes founded on pride, which derive glory and nourish-

ment out of pain itself; far more suitable are ridicule and infamy—punishments that check the pride of fanatics with the pride of the onlookers, and from the tenacity of which even truth itself can hardly work its way loose, with slow and obstinate efforts. Thus by opposing forces against forces, and opinions against opinions, the wise legislator breaks down the admiration and surprise of the populace occasioned by a false principle, the correctly deduced consequences of which tend to conceal from popular minds the original absurdity.

The punishments of infamy should neither be too frequent nor fall upon a great number of persons at one time—not the first, because the true and too often repeated effects of matters of opinion weaken the force of opinion itself, and not the second, because the infamy of many resolves itself into the infamy of none.

This is the way to avoid confounding the relations and the invariable nature of things, which, not being limited by time and operating incessantly, confounds and overturns all limited regulations that stray from its course. It is not only the arts of taste and pleasure that have as their universal principle the faithful imitation of nature, but politics itself, at least that which is true and lasting, is subject to this universal maxim, for it is nothing other than the art of properly directing and co-ordinating the immutable sentiments of men.

XIX

PROMPTNESS OF PUNISHMENT

The more promptly and the more closely punishment follows upon the commission of a crime, the more just and useful will it be. I say more just, because the criminal is thereby spared the useless and cruel torments of uncertainty, which increase with the vigor of imagination and with the sense of personal weakness; more just, because privation of liberty, being itself a punishment, should not precede the sentence except when necessity requires. Imprisonment of a citizen, then, is simply custody of his person until he be judged guilty; and this custody, being essentially penal, should be of the least possible duration and of the least possible severity. The time limit should be determined both by the anticipated length of the trial and by seniority among those who are entitled to be tried first. The strictness of confinement should be no more than is necessary to prevent him from taking flight or from concealing the proofs of his crimes. The trial itself should be completed in the briefest possible time. What crueler contrast than the indolence of a judge and the anguish of a man under accusation—the comforts and pleasures of an insensitive magistrate on one side, and on the other the tears, the squalor of a prisoner? In general, the weight of punishment and the consequence of a crime should be that which is most efficacious for others, and which inflicts the least possible hardship upon the person who suffers it; one cannot call legitimate any society which does not maintain, as an infallible principle, that men have wished to subject themselves only to the least possible evils.

I have said that the promptness of punishments is more useful because when the length of time that passes between the punishment and the misdeed is less, so much the stronger and more lasting in the human mind is the association of these two ideas, *crime and punishment;* they then come insensibly to be considered, one as the cause, the other as the necessary inevitable effect. It has been demonstrated that the association of ideas is the cement that forms the entire fabric of the human intellect; without this cement pleasure and pain would be isolated sentiments and of no effect. The more men depart from general ideas and universal principles, that is, the more vulgar they are, the more apt are they to act merely on immediate and familiar associations, ignoring the more remote and complex ones that serve only men strongly impassioned for the object of their desires; the light of attention illuminates only a single object, leaving the others dark. They are of service also to more elevated minds, for they have acquired the habit of rapidly surveying many objects at once, and are able with facility to contrast many partial sentiments one with another, so that the result, which is action, is less dangerous and uncertain.

Of utmost importance is it, therefore, that the crime and the punishment be intimately linked together, if it be desirable that, in crude, vulgar minds, the seductive picture of a particularly advantageous crime should immediately call up the associated idea of punishment. Long delay always produces the effect of further separating these two ideas; thus, though punishment of a crime may make an impression, it will be less as a punishment than as a spectacle, and will be felt only after the horror of the particular crime, which should serve to reinforce the feeling of punishment, has been much weakened in the hearts of the spectators.

Another principle serves admirably to draw even closer the important connection between a misdeed and its punishment, namely, that the latter be as much in conformity as possible with the nature of the crime. This analogy facilitates admirably the contrast that ought to exist between the inducement to crime and the counterforce of punishment, so that the latter may deter and lead the mind toward a goal the very opposite of that toward which the seductive idea of breaking the laws seeks to direct it.

Those guilty of lesser crimes are usually punished either in the obscurity of a prison or by transportation, to serve as an example, with a distant and therefore almost useless servitude, to nations which they have not offended. Since men are not induced on the spur of the moment to commit the gravest crimes, public punishment of a great misdeed will be regarded by the majority as something very remote and of improbable occurrence; but public punishment of lesser crimes, which are closer to men's hearts, will make an impression which, while deterring them from these, deters them even further from the graver crimes. A proportioning of punishments to one another and to crimes should comprehend not only their force but also the manner of inflicting them.

XX

THE CERTAINTY OF PUNISHMENT.
MERCY

One of the greatest curbs on crimes is not the cruelty of
punishments, but their infallibility, and, consequently, the vigilance of magistrates, and that severity of an inexorable judge
which, to be a useful virtue, must be accompanied by a mild
legislation. The certainty of a punishment, even if it be moderate, will always make a stronger impression than the fear of
another which is more terrible but combined with the hope of
impunity; even the least evils, when they are certain, always
terrify men's minds, and hope, that heavenly gift which is often
our sole recompense for everything, tends to keep the thought
of greater evils remote from us, especially when its strength
is increased by the idea of impunity which avarice and weakness only too often afford.

Sometimes a man is freed from punishment for a lesser
crime when the offended party chooses to forgive—an act in
accord with beneficence and humanity, but contrary to the
public good—as if a private citizen, by an act of remission,
could eliminate the need for an example, in the same way
that he can waive compensation for the injury. The right to
inflict punishment is a right not of an individual, but of all
citizens, or of their sovereign. An individual can renounce his
own portion of right, but cannot annul that of others.

As punishments become more mild, clemency and pardon
become less necessary. Happy the nation in which they might
some day be considered pernicious! Clemency, therefore, that
virtue which has sometimes been deemed a sufficient substitute in a sovereign for all the duties of the throne, should be
excluded from perfect legislation, where the punishments are
mild and the method of judgment regular and expeditious.
This truth will seem harsh to anyone living in the midst of
the disorders of a criminal system, where pardons and mercy

are necessary to compensate for the absurdity of the laws and the severity of the sentences. This, which is indeed the noblest prerogative of the throne, the most desirable attribute of sovereignty, is also, however, the tacit disapprobation of the beneficent dispensers of public happiness for a code which, with all its imperfections, has in its favor the prejudice of centuries, the voluminous and imposing dowry of innumerable commentators, the weighty apparatus of endless formalities, and the adherence of the most insinuating and least formidable of the semi-learned. But one ought to consider that clemency is a virtue of the legislators and not of the executors of the laws, that it ought to shine in the code itself rather than in the particular judgments. To make men see that crimes can be pardoned or that punishment is not their necessary consequence foments a flattering hope of impunity and creates a belief that, because they might be remitted, sentences which are not remitted are rather acts of oppressive violence than emanations of justice. What is to be said, then, when the ruler grants pardons, that is, public security to a particular individual, and, with a personal act of unenlightened beneficence, constitutes a public decree of impunity? Let the laws, therefore, be inexorable, and inexorable their executors in particular cases, but let the legislator be tender, indulgent, and humane. Let him, a wise architect, raise his building upon the foundation of self-love and let the general interest be the result of the interests of each; he shall not then be constrained, by partial laws and tumultuous remedies, to separate at every moment the public good from that of individuals, and to build the image of public well-being upon fear and distrust. Wise and compassionate philosopher, let him permit men, his brothers, to enjoy in peace that small portion of happiness which the grand system established by the First Cause, by that *which is,* allows them to enjoy in this corner of the universe.

XXI

ASYLUMS

There remain two other questions for me to examine: one, whether asylums are just, and whether an international pact for reciprocal exchange of criminals is useful or not. Within the confines of a country there should be no place independent of the laws. Their power should pursue every citizen, as the shadow pursues its body. Impunity and asylum differ only in degree, and as the effectiveness of punishment consists more in the certainty of receiving it than in its force, asylums encourage crimes more than punishments deter them. To multiply asylums is to create a multitude of petty sovereignties, for where laws do not effectively command, there new laws may easily be formed opposed to the common ones, and also a spirit opposed to that of the entire body of society. All histories show that asylums have given origin to great revolutions in states and in the opinions of men.

Some persons have maintained that punishment may be meted out for a crime, that is, for an action contrary to the laws, regardless of where it is committed; as if the character of a subject were indelible, that is, synonymous with or rather worse than that of slave; as if a man could be wholly subject to one government while living under another, and as if his actions could, without contradiction, be subordinated to two sovereigns and to two often contradictory codes of laws. Some believe, also, that a cruel act done, for example, in Constantinople, may be punished in Paris, for the abstract reason that one who offends humanity merits the collective enmity of mankind and universal execration—as if judges were the vindicators of the universal sensibility of men, rather than of the pacts that bind them to one another. The place of punishment is the place of the crime, because only there and not elsewhere are men under constraint to injure a private person in order to prevent public injury. A wretch who has not broken the pacts of a society of which he was not a member may be feared and, therefore, by the superior force of society exiled and excluded; but he should not be punished with the formality of the laws, which are vindicators of social compacts, not of the intrinsic malice of human actions.

But, whether international agreements for the reciprocal exchange of criminals be useful, I would not dare to decide until laws more in conformity with the needs of humanity, until milder punishments and an end to dependence on arbitrary power and opinion, have provided security for oppressed innocence and hated virtue—until universal reason, which ever tends the more to unite the interests of throne and subjects, has confined tyranny altogether to the vast plains of Asia, though, undoubtedly, the persuasion that there is not a foot of soil upon which real crimes are pardoned would be a most efficacious means of preventing them.

XXII

REWARDS

The other question is whether it is useful to put a price on the head of a known criminal and to make each citizen an executioner by arming his hand. The criminal is either beyond the borders of his country or within them; in the first case, the sovereign encourages citizens to commit a crime and exposes them to punishment, he himself thereby committing an injury and a usurpation of authority in the dominions of another, and in that way authorizing other nations to do the same to him. In the second case, he displays his own weakness. He who has strength to defend himself will not seek to purchase it. Moreover, such an edict upsets all ideas of morality and virtue, which, at the slightest breath, are apt to vanish from the minds of men. At one time the laws encourage treachery, at another they punish it. With one hand the legislator strengthens the bonds of family, of kindred, of friendship,

and with the other rewards a man for violating and despising
them; always in contradiction with himself, he now invites the
suspicious natures of men into mutual confidence, and now
plants distrust in all hearts. Instead of preventing one crime,
he brings on a hundred. These are the expedients of weak
nations, whose laws are but the temporary repairs of a ruined
edifice which crumbles in all parts. To the extent that a nation becomes more enlightened, honesty and mutual confidence
become necessary, and tend always to identify themselves the
more with sound policy. Schemes and intrigues, dark and indirect ways, are for the most part foreseen, and the sensibility
of all counterbalances that of particular individuals. Even the
ages of ignorance, in which public morality inclines men to
live by private standards, serve as instruction and experience
for enlightened ages. But the laws that reward treachery and
excite clandestine war, scattering reciprocal suspicion among
citizens, oppose this very necessary union of morality and politics to which men would owe their happiness, nations their
peace, and the universe some longer interval of tranquility
and of rest from the evils that run to and fro in it.

XXIII

PROPORTION BETWEEN CRIMES AND PUNISHMENTS

It is to the common interest not only that crimes not be
committed, but also that they be less frequent in proportion
to the harm they cause society. Therefore, the obstacles that
deter men from committing crimes should be stronger in proportion as they are contrary to the public good, and as the
inducements to commit them are stronger. There must, therefore, be a proper proportion between crimes and punishments.[36]

[36] [Cf. Montesquieu, *Spirit*, VI, 16: "It is an essential point that there
should be a certain proportion in punishments, because it is essential

If pleasure and pain are the motives of sensible beings, if, among the motives for even the sublimest acts of men, rewards and punishments were designated by the invisible Legislator, from their inexact distribution arises the contradiction, as little observed as it is common, that the punishments punish crimes which they themselves have occasioned. If an equal punishment be ordained for two crimes that do not equally injure society, men will not be any more deterred from committing the greater crime, if they find a greater advantage associated with it.

Whoever sees the same death penalty, for instance, decreed for the killing of a pheasant and for the assassination of a man or for forgery of an important writing, will make no distinction between such crimes, thereby destroying the moral sentiments, which are the work of many centuries and of much blood, slowly and with great difficulty registered in the human spirit, and impossible to produce, many believe, without the aid of the most sublime of motives and of an enormous apparatus of grave formalities.

It is impossible to prevent all disorders in the universal conflict of human passions. They increase according to a ratio compounded of population and the crossings of particular interests, which cannot be directed with geometric precision to the public utility. For mathematical exactitude we must substitute, in the arithmetic of politics, the calculation of probabilities. A glance at the histories will show that disorders increase with the confines of empires. National sentiment declining in the same proportion, the tendency to commit crimes increases with the increased interest everyone takes in such disorders; thus there is a constantly increasing need to make punishments heavier.

That force, similar to gravity, which impels us to seek our own well-being is restrained in its operation only to the extent that obstacles are set up against it. The effects of this force are the confused series of human actions. If these clash

that a great crime should be avoided rather than a smaller, and that which is more pernicious to society rather than that which is less."]

together and disturb one another, punishments, which I would call "political obstacles," prevent the bad effect without destroying the impelling cause, which is that sensibility inseparable from man. And the legislator acts then like an able architect whose function it is to check the destructive tendencies of gravity and to align correctly those that contribute to the strength of the building.

Given the necessity of human association, given the pacts that result from the very opposition of private interests, a scale of disorders is distinguishable, the first grade consisting of those that are immediately destructive of society, and the last, of those that do the least possible injustice to its individual members. Between these extremes are included all the actions contrary to the public good that are called crimes, and they all descend by insensible gradations from the highest to the lowest. If geometry were applicable to the infinite and obscure combinations of human actions, there ought to be a corresponding scale of punishments, descending from the greatest to the least; if there were an exact and universal scale of punishments and of crimes, we would have a fairly reliable and common measure of the degrees of tyranny and liberty, of the fund of humanity or of malice, of the various nations. But it is enough for the wise legislator to mark the principal points of division without disturbing the order, not assigning to crimes of the first grade the punishments of the last.

XXIV

THE MEASURE OF CRIMES

We have seen what the true measure of crimes is—namely, the *harm done to society*. This is one of those palpable truths which, though requiring neither quadrants nor telescopes for their discovery, and lying well within the capacity of any ordinary intellect, are, nevertheless, because of a marvelous combination of circumstances, known with clarity and precision only by some few thinking men in every nation and in every age. But notions of an Asiatic sort, and passions clothed with authority and power, usually with indiscernible but sometimes with violent impressions made on the timid credulity of men, have effaced the simple notions that perhaps formed the first philosophy of primitive societies—notions back to which the present enlightenment seems to be leading us, but with that greater degree of certitude obtainable through precise analysis, through a thousand unhappy experiences and from the very obstacles in its way.

They were in error who believed that the true measure of crimes is to be found in the intention of the person who commits them. Intention depends on the impression objects actually make and on the precedent disposition of the mind; these vary in all men and in each man, according to the swift succession of ideas, of passions, and of circumstances. It would be necessary, therefore, to form not only a particular code for each citizen, but a new law for every crime. Sometimes, with the best intentions, men do the greatest injury to society; at other times, intending the worst for it, they do the greatest good.

Others measure crimes rather by the dignity of the injured person than by the importance [of the offense] with respect to the public good. If this were the true measure of crimes, an irreverence toward the Being of beings ought to be more severely punished than the assassination of a monarch, the superiority of nature constituting infinite compensation for the difference in the injury.

Finally, some have thought that the gravity of sinfulness ought to enter into the measure of crimes. The fallacy of this opinion will at once appear to the eye of an impartial examiner of the true relations between men and men, and between men and God. The first are relations of equality. Necessity alone brought into being, out of the clash of passions and the opposition of interests, the idea of *common utility*, which is the foundation of human justice. The second are relations of dependence on a perfect Being and Creator, who has reserved to himself alone the right to be legislator and judge at the same time, because he alone can be such without inconvenience. If he has established eternal punishments for anyone who disobeys his omnipotence, what insect is it that shall dare to take the place of divine justice, that shall want to vindicate the Being who is sufficient unto himself, who cannot receive from things any impression of pleasure or pain, and who, alone among all beings, acts without suffering any reaction? The weight of sin depends on the inscrutable malice of the heart, which can be known by finite beings only if it is revealed. How then can a norm for punishing crimes be drawn from this? Men might in such a case punish where God forgives, and forgive where God punishes. If men can be in opposition with the Omnipotent in offending him, they may also be so in punishing.

XXV

THE CLASSIFICATION OF CRIMES

Some crimes directly destroy society, or the person who represents it; some injure the private security of a citizen in his life, in his goods, or in his honor; some others are actions contrary to what everyone is supposed to do or not do in view of the public good.

Any action not included between the two extremes indicated above cannot be called a "crime," or be punished as such, except by those who find their interest in applying that name. The uncertainty of these limits has produced, in nations, a morality that contradicts legislation, a number of actual legislative systems that are mutually exclusive, a host of laws that expose the wisest to the severest punishments. Thus are the terms "vice" and "virtue" rendered vague and fluctuating, and there emerges that sense of uncertainty about one's own existence which produces the lethargy and sleep that is fatal to political communities.

The view that each citizen should have it within his power to do all that is not contrary to the laws, without having to fear any other inconvenience than that which may result from the action itself—this is the political dogma that should be believed by the people and inculcated by the supreme magistrates, with the incorruptible guardianship of the laws. [It is] a sacred dogma without which there can be no lawful society; a just recompense to men for their sacrifice of that universal liberty of action over all things, which is the property of every sensible being, limited only by its own powers. This shapes free and vigorous souls and enlightened minds; this makes men virtuous with that virtue which can resist fear, and not that of pliant prudence, worthy only of those who can endure a precarious and uncertain existence.

Anyone who will read with a philosophic eye the codes of nations and their annals will generally find the designations of "vice" and "virtue," of "good citizen" or "criminal," changing in the course of centuries, not because of the transformations that occur in the circumstances of countries, which, consequently, always accord with the common interest, but because of the passions and errors that have successively swayed the different legislators. He will frequently remark that the passions of one century are the basis for the morality of future centuries —that strong passions, offspring of fanaticism and enthusiasm, weakened and corroded, so to speak, by time (which reduces all physical and moral phenomena to equilibrium), gradually become the prudence of the age, and a useful tool in the hand of the strong and artful. In this way, those extremely vague notions of honor and virtue have come into being, and they are such because they change with the course of time which enables names to outlive things; they change with the rivers and mountains, which quite often form the confines not only of physical but also of moral geography.

XXVI

CRIMES OF LESE MAJESTY

The first class of crimes, which are the gravest because most injurious, are those known as crimes of lese majesty [high treason]. Only tyranny and ignorance, confounding the clearest terms and ideas, can apply this name and consequently the gravest punishment, to crimes of a different nature, thereby making men, on this as on a thousand other occasions, victims of a word. Every crime, even of a private nature, injures society, but it is not every crime that aims at its immediate destruction. Moral as well as physical actions have their limited sphere of activity, and are diversely circumscribed, like all movements of nature, by time and space; therefore only sophistical interpretation, which is usually the philosophy of slavery, can confound the immutable relations of things distinguished by eternal truth.

XXVII

CRIMES AGAINST PERSONAL SECURITY. ACTS OF VIOLENCE. PUNISHMENTS OF NOBLES

After these come the crimes against the security of individual citizens. Inasmuch as this is the primary end of all political association, some of the severest of punishments established by law must be assigned to any violation of the right of security acquired by every citizen.

Some crimes are attempts against the person, others against property. The penalties for the first should always be corporal punishments. MEANING WHAT?

Attempts against the security and liberty of citizens are among the greatest of crimes. Within this class are included not only the assassinations and thefts committed by men of the lower classes but also those committed by noblemen and magistrates, the example of which acts with greater force and is more far-reaching, destroying the ideas of justice and duty among subjects and substituting that of the right of the strongest, equally dangerous, in the end, to those who exercise it and to those who suffer it.

The great and rich should not have it in their power to set a price upon attempts made against the weak and the poor; otherwise riches, which are, under the laws, the reward of industry, become the nourishment of tyranny. There is no liberty whenever the laws permit that, in some circumstances, a man can cease to be a *person* and become a *thing;* then you will see all the industry of the powerful person applied to extract from the mass of social interrelations whatever the law allows in his favor. This discovery is the magic secret that changes citizens into beasts of burden; in the hands of the strong, it is the chain with which he fetters the activities of the incautious and weak. This is the reason why, in certain governments that have all the appearances of liberty, tyranny lies hidden or introduces itself, unseen, in some corner neglected by the legislator, where, imperceptibly, it acquires power and grows large.

Men generally set up the most solid embankments against open tyranny, but do not see the imperceptible insect that gnaws at them and opens to the flooding stream a way that is more secure because more hidden.

What punishments, then, shall the crimes of nobles merit, whose privileges form so great a part of the laws of nations? I shall not here inquire whether this hereditary distinction between nobles and commoners is useful in a government, or necessary in a monarchy, or whether it be true that they form an intermediary power which limits the excesses of the two extremes, and not, rather, a class which, slave to itself and to others, confines all movement of trust and of hope within an extremely narrow circle, like those fertile and pleasant little oases that stand out in the vast desert sands of Arabia; or whether, even admitting that inequality is inevitable, or useful, in societies, it be true also that it should subsist between classes rather than individuals, confine itself in one place rather than circulate throughout the body politic, perpetuate itself rather than renew and destroy itself incessantly. I shall limit myself to considering only the punishments to be assigned to noblemen, asserting that they should be the same for the first as for the least citizen. Every legitimate distinction, whether in honors or in riches, presupposes an original equality founded on the laws, which consider all subjects as equally dependent upon them. It is to be supposed that men, in renouncing their natural despotism, have said: "The more industrious person shall have the greater honors, and his fame shall reflect upon his successors; but while he who is happier or more honored can hope for more, let him fear no less than the others to violate those pacts by which he is raised above others." It is true that such decrees have not emanated from any diet of all mankind, yet they exist in the invariable relations of things; they do not destroy the advantages allegedly produced by nobility, but they prevent the inconveniences; they inspire respect for the laws by closing every way to impunity. To the objection that the same punishment inflicted on a nobleman and a plebeian is not really the same because of the diversity of their education, and because of the disgrace that is spread over an illustrious family, I would answer that the measure of punishments is not the sensibility of the criminal, but the public injury, which is all the more grave when committed by a person of rank; that equality of punishments can only be extrinsic, since in reality the effect on each individual is diverse; that the disgrace of a family may be removed by the sovereign through public demonstration of benevolence toward the innocent relatives of the criminal. And who does not know that external formalities take the place of reason for the credulous and admiring populace?

XXVIII

INJURIES TO HONOR

Personal injuries that detract from honor, that is, from the just portion of esteem which one citizen has the right to exact from others, should be punished with disgrace [*infamia*].

There is a remarkable contradiction between the civil laws, those jealous guardians, above all, of the life and property of each citizen, and the laws of what is called "honor," which respects opinion above everything else. This word "honor" has served as a basis for many long and brilliant argumentations, without contributing a single fixed and stable idea. A miserable condition it is indeed, for human minds, that the most remote and least important ideas about the revolutions of heavenly bodies should be more immediately and distinctly known than the near and very important notions of morality, which are always fluctuating and confused, as they are borne about by the winds of passion and as they are received and transmitted by practiced ignorance. But the semblance of paradox will vanish if it be considered that just as objects, when too close to the eyes, become confused, so the exceeding nearness of moral ideas causes a mixing together of the many simple ideas that compose them, and thus there is a confounding of the line of separation required by the geometric spirit which strives to measure exactly the phenomena of human sensibility. And grounds for amazement will disappear completely in the impartial student of human affairs, who may entertain a suspicion that perhaps neither so great an apparatus of morality nor so many ties are necessary for the happiness and security of mankind.

Honor, then, is one of those complex ideas which are an aggregate not only of simple ones but of ideas equally complex which in the various aspects they present to the mind now admit and now exclude some of the diverse elements that compose them, retaining only a few of their common ideas, just

as many complex algebraic quantities admit one common
divisor. To find this common divisor of the various ideas that
men form of *honor*, it is necessary to glance back rapidly to
the formation of societies.

The first laws and the first magistrates originated from the
need to remedy the disorders produced by the natural despotism of individuals; this was the end for which society was instituted and this primary end has always been maintained
either actually or apparently at the head of all codes, even the
destructive ones. But closer association of men and the ad-
vancement of their learning have given origin to an infinite
series of activities and reciprocal needs lying always beyond
the foresight of the laws, and just short of the actual power
of each individual. From this epoch began the despotism of
opinion which was the only means for obtaining advantages
and averting evils for which the laws were not sufficient to
provide. Opinion it is that torments both the wise and the
vulgar, that has credited the appearance of virtue above virtue
itself, that makes even a scoundrel turn missionary because he
finds his own interest in it. Hence the esteem of men became
not only useful but necessary to keep from sinking below the
common level. Hence, if the ambitious man strives to gain it
as useful, if the vain person goes begging for it as a testimony
of his personal merit, the man of honor is found exacting it as
a necessity. This *honor* is a condition which many men place
on their own existence. Having come into being after the formation of society, it could not be placed in the common depository; it is, rather, a temporary return to the state of nature,
a momentary withdrawal of one's own person from the laws,
which, in that case, do not sufficiently protect a citizen.

Hence, in extreme political liberty and in extreme subjection, the laws of honor disappear or become altogether confounded with the others; for, in the first case, the despotism
of the laws renders the quest for the esteem of others useless;
in the second, the despotism of men, nullifying civil existence,
reduces everyone to a precarious and momentary personality.
Honor is, therefore, one of the fundamental principles of those

monarchies in which rule is a limited form of despotism [37]; it
is in them what revolutions are in despotic states—a momentary return to the state of nature, reminding the ruler of the
original condition of equality.

XXIX

DUELS

From this need for the esteem of others arose private duels,
which originated precisely in the anarchy of the laws. It is
alleged that they were unknown in antiquity, perhaps because
the ancients did not assemble, suspiciously armed, in the temples, in the theaters and with friends, perhaps because the duel
was an ordinary and common spectacle offered as public en-
tertainment by vile and slavish gladiators, and because freemen
disdained to be thought and called gladiators because of private combats. Edicts imposing the death penalty on all who
accept challenges have failed to extirpate this custom which
is founded on what some men fear more than death. When deprived of the esteem of others the man of honor sees himself
exposed either to become a merely solitary being, an insuffer-
able state for a social man, or else to become a butt of insults
and infamy, which, by their repetition, overcome the fear of
punishment. Why do common people, for the most part, duel
less than the grand? Not only because they are disarmed, but
because the need for the esteem of others is less general among
the commoners than among those who, being of higher rank,
regard themselves with greater suspicion and jealousy.

It is not useless to repeat what has been written by others—
that the best method of preventing this crime is to punish the
aggressor, namely, the one who has given occasion for the

---

[37] [Cf. Montesquieu, *Spirit*, III, 8: "Honor is far from being the principle of despotic government: mankind being here all upon a level, no one
person can prefer himself to another, and as on the other hand they
are all slaves, they can give themselves no sort of preference."]

duel, and to acquit him who, without personal fault, has been obliged to defend what the existing laws do not assure him, that is, opinion.[38]

XXX

THEFTS

Thefts not involving violence should be punished by a fine. Whoever seeks to enrich himself at the expense of others should be deprived of his own. But, since this is ordinarily the crime only of poverty and desperation, the crime of that unhappy portion of mankind to whom the right of property (a terrible and perhaps unnecessary right [39]) has left but a bare existence, and since pecuniary punishments increase the number of criminals beyond that of the crimes, and since they deprive innocent persons of bread while taking it from rascals, the most suitable punishment will be that kind of servitude which alone can be called just—the temporary subjection of the labors and person of the criminal to the community, as repayment, through total personal dependence, for the unjust despotism usurped against the social contract. But when the theft involves violence, punishment also should be a mixture of the corporeal and servile. Other writers have shown the evident disorder that arises from not distinguishing the punishments for assault and robbery from those for simple theft, thus making an absurd equation between a great sum of money and a man's life. These are crimes of a different nature, and in politics no less than in mathematics the axiom holds which says that heterogeneous quantities are separated by infinity itself. It

[38] [Reputation. The good opinion of others.]

[39] [Cesare Cantù informs us, in *Beccaria e il Diritto Penale* (Firenze, 1862), p. 127, note a, that in a manuscript of Beccaria's own hand as well as in the first edition, Beccaria had written "a terrible but perhaps necessary right"—that is to say, quite the opposite of "a terrible and perhaps unnecessary right," as found here.]

is never superfluous to repeat what has almost never been put into practice. Political machinery, more than all others, retains the initial impetus given to it and is slowest in acquiring a new one.

XXXI

SMUGGLING

Smuggling is a real crime that injures both the sovereign and the nation, but its punishment should not involve infamy for it is itself not infamous in public opinion. But why is it that no disgrace attends the commission of this crime, which is after all a theft against the ruler and, as a consequence, against the nation? I answer that offenses which men believe cannot be committed against them do not interest them sufficiently to excite public indignation against those who commit them. Smuggling is such an offense. Most men, upon whom remote consequences make very weak impressions, do not see the damage that can result from smuggling. In fact, they often enjoy the present advantages of it. They see only the damage done to the prince. They are, then, less interested in refusing esteem to a smuggler than to persons who commit a private theft, forgery of signatures, and other evils that they themselves may suffer. The principle is, evidently, that every sensitive being is interested only in the evils with which he is acquainted.

This crime arises from the law itself, for the higher the custom duty, the greater the advantage; thus the temptation and facility of smuggling increases with the boundaries to be guarded and with the reduced bulk of the prohibited merchandise. Seizure of both the prescribed goods and whatever accompanies it is a very just punishment. But it would be more efficacious if the custom duty were less, for men take risks only in proportion to the advantage to be derived from success in their undertaking.

But should such a crime go unpunished when committed by someone who has nothing to lose? No: smuggling in some cases so affects the public revenue (that very essential and very difficult part of a good legislative system) that it deserves a considerable punishment, even imprisonment itself, or penal servitude, but imprisonment and servitude conforming to the nature of the crime itself. For example, the imprisonment meted out to a tobacco smuggler should not be the same as that assigned to an assassin or thief; his labors, if limited to the work and service of the royal treasury he meant to defraud, will then be most conformable to the nature of the punishments.

XXXII

DEBTORS

The good faith of contracts, the security of commerce, oblige the legislator to secure for creditors the persons of bankrupt debtors. But I think it important to distinguish between the fraudulent and the innocent bankrupt: the first should be assigned the same punishment that counterfeiters of money receive, for to counterfeit a piece of coined metal, which is a pledge of the obligations of citizens, is not a greater crime than to counterfeit the obligations themselves. But the innocent bankrupt, who, after a rigorous examination, has demonstrated before his judge that either the malice or the misfortune of others, or events which human prudence cannot avoid, have stripped him of his possessions—upon what barbarous pretense is he thrown into prison, deprived of the sole sad good that yet remains to him, that of mere liberty, to experience the agonies of the guilty, and, perhaps, with the desperation of violated honesty, to repent of the very innocence that permitted him to live peacefully under the tutelage of those laws which it was not in his power not to offend?—laws dictated by the powerful out of greed and suffered by the weak for the sake of that hope glittering now and then in the human heart, which makes us believe that unlucky accidents are reserved for others and only advantageous ones for us? Men, left to the sway of their most obvious feelings, love cruel laws, even though, being subject to the same themselves, it is to their own interest that they should be mild, since the fear of being injured is greater than the desire to injure.

Again, concerning the innocent bankrupt, I say that, though there be no cancellation of his obligation short of full payment, though he be refused the liberty of removing himself without the consent of the interested parties and of subjecting to other laws his own industry, which should under penalty be employed to enable him to render satisfaction in proportion to his earnings, what legal pretext can there be, like the security of commerce, like the sacred right of property, that could justify a privation of liberty, of no use at all, except if it were a case of revealing through the evils of servitude the secrets of an allegedly innocent bankrupt—a rare case indeed, assuming there has been a rigorous inquiry? I think it to be a legislative maxim that the importance of political inconvenience is determinable as a ratio varying directly with the public injury and inversely with the probability of its verification.

One might distinguish actual fraud from a grave fault, and grave from light, and this from perfect innocence; and by assigning to the first the punishments for crimes of forgery, to the second, lesser punishments, but with loss of liberty, and by reserving for the last a free choice of the means of restitution, one might deprive the third of liberty to do so, leaving it to his creditors. But the distinctions between grave and light should be fixed by the blind and impartial laws and not by the dangerous and arbitrary prudence of judges. Fixing of limits is as necessary in politics as in mathematics, not less in measuring the public good than in measuring size.[40]

40 Commerce and private property are not an end of the social contract but they may be a means for attaining such an end. To expose all the members of society to evils which so many circumstances are apt to produce would be a subordinating of ends to means—a paralogism of all the

With what ease might a far-seeing legislator prevent the greater part of fraudulent bankruptcies and relieve the misfortunes of the industrious and innocent! Public and open registration of all contracts, and liberty for all citizens to consult the well-ordered documents, a public bank formed out of intelligently apportioned revenues derived from a prosperous commerce and designed to provide timely financial assistance for any unfortunate and innocent member would occasion no real inconvenience and might produce innumerable advantages. But the easy, simple, and grand laws that await only the nod of the legislator to diffuse wealth and strength through the body of a nation, laws that would gain for him everlasting hymns of gratitude from generation upon generation, are either least of all known or least desired. A restless and trifling spirit, the timid prudence of the present moment, a distrustful rigidity against innovation overpower the feelings of those who manage the maze of activities of petty mortals.

XXXIII

PUBLIC TRANQUILITY

Lastly, among crimes of the third kind are to be included particularly those that disturb the public tranquility and the quiet of citizens, such as cries and upheavals in public streets intended for traffic and the strolling of citizens, or fanatical sermons that excite the easy passions of the curious multitude, gathering force from the crowding of listeners, and more from

---

sciences and especially of the political, into which I fell in the preceding editions, where I said that the innocent bankrupt should be kept in custody as a pledge of his debts or employed as a slave to work for his creditors. I am ashamed of having so written. I have been accused of impiety, and should not have been. I have been accused of sedition and should not have been. I offended the rights of humanity, and no one has reproached me for it!

obscure and mysterious enthusiasm than from clear and quiet reason, which never has any effect upon a great mass of men.

The night illuminated at public expense, guards stationed in the various quarters of the city, the simple and moral discourses of religion confined to the silence and to the sacred quiet of temples protected by public authority, harangues in support of private and public interests delivered in the assemblies of the nation, in the parliaments, or where the majesty of the sovereign resides—all are efficacious means for preventing any dangerous fermentation of popular passions. Together they form a principal branch of magisterial vigilance which the French call "police"; but if this magistracy should operate by means of arbitrary laws, not established by a code currently in the hands of all citizens, the door is open to tyranny which always surrounds the confines of political liberty. I find no exception to this general axiom, that every citizen should know when he is guilty of crime and when he is innocent. If censors and, in general, arbitrary magistrates are necessary in any government, the reason lies in the weakness in its constitution and not in the nature of well-ordered government. Uncertainty regarding their lot has sacrificed more victims to secret tyranny than have ever suffered from public and solemn cruelty. It inspires revulsion more than it vilifies. The true tyrant always begins by ruling over opinion, thus forestalling courage which can only shine forth in the clear light of truth, in the heat of passions, or in ignorance of danger.

XXXIV

POLITICAL INDOLENCE

Wise governments do not tolerate political indolence in the midst of work and industry. By political indolence I mean the kind which contributes nothing to society either by its work or its wealth, which acquires without ever losing, which the

vulgar regard with stupid adoration and the wise with disdainful compassion for the beings who are its victims, which, lacking the incitement to active life that is necessary to protect or
to increase its commodities, leaves to the passions of opinion,
strong as they are, all their energy. This kind of indolence has
been confused by austere moralists with the indolence of riches
accumulated by industry; yet it is not the austere and limited
virtue of a few censors but the laws that should define what
sort of indolence is to be punished. He is not in the political
sense indolent who enjoys the fruits of the vices or virtues of
his own ancestors, providing, in exchange for immediate pleasures, bread and existence for industrious poverty, who carries
on in peace the tacit war of indolence with opulence, instead
of the uncertain and bloody one with force. Such indolence is
necessary and useful to the degree that society expands and its
administration contracts.

XXXV

SUICIDE AND EXPATRIATION

Suicide seems to be a crime that admits of no punishment in
the true sense, since it can only fall upon innocent persons or
upon a cold and insensible body. If the latter is apt to impress
the living no more than would the flaying of a statue, the
former is unjust and tyrannical, for political liberty in men
requires of necessity that punishments be merely personal. Men
love life exceedingly and all that surrounds them strengthens
them in this love. The seductive image of pleasure and of hope,
sweetest beguiler of mortals, for the sake of which we swallow
large draughts of evil mixed with but a few drops of content-
ment, allures men too much, so that one need never fear that
the necessary impunity of such a crime should have much influence upon them. Whoever fears pain obeys the laws; but
death extinguishes in a body all sources of pain. What motive,
then, is to restrain the desperate hand of the suicide?

A person who kills himself does less injury to society than one who abandons its confines forever; the former leaves his entire substance there, while the latter removes himself together with part of his possessions. Indeed, if the strength of a community consists in the number of citizens, by withdrawing and transferring himself to a neighboring nation [the expatriate] does a double injury as compared with [the suicide] who, by means of death, removes himself from society. The question therefore reduces itself to knowing whether it is useful or injurious to a nation to allow its members perpetual freedom to live beyond its borders.

No law should be promulgated that lacks force or that the nature of the circumstances renders ineffectual; and as men are swayed by opinion, which obeys the slow and indirect impressions of the legislator, while resisting the direct and violent, so useless laws, which are despised by men, communicate their meanness even to the most salutary laws, which are then regarded as an obstacle to be overcome rather than as the deposit of public good.

Indeed, if, as was said, our sentiments are limited, the more respect men have for things beyond the laws, the less can they have for the laws themselves. From this principle the wise administrator of public happiness may draw some useful consequences which, were I to expound them, would take me too far from my subject, which is to prove the uselessness of making a prison of the state. A law to that effect is useless because, except where inaccessible cliffs or unnavigable seas separate a nation from all others, how are all points of its circumference to be closed? And who will guard the guards? A man who carries everything away with him, precisely because he has done so, cannot be punished. Once committed, such a crime can no longer be punished, and to punish it beforehand is to punish the will of men and not their action; it is an attempt to regulate the intentions, the freest part of man, altogether beyond the sway of human laws. To punish an expatriate in the substance he has left behind, even omitting from consideration the facility and inevitability of collusion which could not be prevented without tyrannizing over contracts, would reduce to nothing all commerce between nations. To punish the criminal on his return would be to prevent reparation of the harm done to society, for it would amount to rendering all absences perpetual. Any prohibition against leaving a country only increases the desire of the nationals to do so, and serves as a warning to foreigners not to enter.

What must we think of a government that has no means other than fear for keeping men in the country to which they have been naturally attached since the earliest impressions of infancy? The surest way to keep citizens in their country is to increase the relative well-being of each of them. Just as every effort ought to be made to turn the balance of trade in our favor, so it is in the greatest interest of the sovereign and of the nation that the sum of happiness, compared with that of surrounding nations, be greater than elsewhere. The pleasures of luxury are not the principal element of this happiness, though they are a necessary remedy for the inequality that increases with a nation's progress, and are indispensable for preventing the concentration of riches in the hands of a single person.[41]

[41] Where the boundaries of a nation increase at a greater rate than its population, there luxury favors despotism; when men are scarcer industry is proportionately less, and when industry is less, poverty is more dependent on extravagance and there is greater difficulty and less to fear in the gatherings of the oppressed against their oppressors. Another reason is that the ceremonial, respects, services, distinctions, and tributes that render more apparent the distance between the strong and the weak, are more easily obtained from few than from many—men being more independent when less observed and much less observed when more numerous. But where the population increases at a greater rate than the boundaries, luxury opposes despotism, because it spurs human industry and activity; popular need offers the rich so many other pleasures and conveniences that they readily forego those of pure ostentation, which add to the sense of independence. Thus it may be observed that in vast, weak, and sparsely populated states, if no other causes interfere, the luxury of ostentation prevails over that of convenience; but in the states that are more populous than vast, the luxury of convenience always causes a diminution of that of ostentation.

But the traffic and trade of the pleasures of luxury has this inconvenience, that, although many persons are involved in carrying it on, it begins and ends in a few and only a tiny part is ever enjoyed by the majority of people, so that it does not relieve the feeling of misery which depends more on comparison than on reality. But personal security and freedom limited only by the laws are what constitute the true foundation of such happiness: accompanied by these the pleasures of luxury favor the population, while without them, they become the instrument of tyranny. As the noblest of animals and the freest of birds retire into solitudes and inaccessible woods, abandoning to insidious man the fertile and smiling plains, so men fly from pleasures themselves when the hand of tyranny offers them.

It is, thus, demonstrated that the law which imprisons subjects in their own country is useless and unjust. Punishment for suicide, then, must be equally so; therefore, although it is a fault that God may punish because he alone can punish after death, it is not a crime in man's eyes, for man's punishment, instead of falling on the criminal himself, falls on his family. To the objection that consideration of such a punishment might, nevertheless, keep a determined man from actually killing himself, my reply is that anyone who calmly renounces the advantage of life, who so hates existence here as to prefer an eternity of unhappiness, is not in the least likely to be moved by the less efficacious and more distant consideration of children and relatives.

XXXVI

CRIMES OF DIFFICULT PROOF

There are some crimes that are at the same time of frequent occurrence in society and yet difficult to prove. Adultery, pederasty, and infanticide are among them.

Adultery is a crime which, considered politically, derives its force and its direction from two causes: the variable laws of men and that very strong attraction that draws one sex toward the other.[42]

Were I to speak to nations still lacking the light of religion, I would say that there is yet another considerable difference between adultery and other crimes. It derives from the abuse of a need that is constant and universal for all humanity—a need that is anterior to, indeed, rather the very foundation of, society itself, whereas other crimes that tend to destroy society owe their origin to momentary passions rather than to natural need. The intensity of such a need seems to those who know something of history and of mankind always to be fixed at the same level in the same climate. Were this so, law and customs designed to diminish the sum total would be not only useless but pernicious, for their effect would be to burden some persons with their own needs and those of others. On the contrary, those laws would be truly wise which by following the easy inclination of the plain, so to speak, would tend to divide and ramify the sum in so many equal and small portions so as to impede uniformly, on all sides, both aridity and inundation. Conjugal fidelity is always proportionate to the number and the liberty of marriages. Where hereditary prejudices govern them, where domestic power arranges them and dissolves them, there gallantry secretly breaks their ties, in spite of vulgar morality, which declaims dutifully against the effects while pardoning the causes. But such reflections are unnecessary for those who, imbued with true religion, are prompted by more sublime motives that correct the force of natural effects. The criminal act itself, in this case, is so instantaneous and mysterious, so concealed by that veil which

[42] This attraction is similar in many respects to the force of gravity which moves the universe; for this, like the other, diminishes with distance; as one regulates all the movements of bodies, so the other, while its period lasts, regulates most of those of the spirit. The dissimilarity consists in this, that while gravity enters into a state of equilibrium with obstructions, the other gathers force and vigor with the increase of obstacles in its way.

the very laws have placed over it (a necessary veil, but so transparent as to enhance rather than diminish the desirability of the thing), the occasions for it are so easy, the consequences so equivocal, that it is more within the power of the legislator to prevent than to correct it. A general rule: when a crime is of such a nature that it must frequently go unpunished, the penalty assigned becomes an incentive. It is a property of our imagination that difficulties, if not insurmountable or too difficult with respect to the natural indolence of a particular individual, excite the imagination more vividly and enlarge the proportions of the object; they are, as it were, so many barriers that confine the erratic and mutable imagination to its object, and, forced as it is to envelop the whole, it attaches itself closely to the agreeable part, toward which our spirit is more naturally inclined, rather than to the painful and injurious, from which it shrinks away as far as possible.

The crime of pederasty, so severely punished by the laws and so easily subjected to the torments that triumph over innocence, is less founded upon the needs of the isolated and independent man than upon the passions of man in society and slavery. It acquires its force not so much from the satiety of pleasures as from that education which, to make men useful to others, begins by making them useless to themselves. It is the work of households where ardent youth is restricted, where, kept by an insurmountable barrier from every other kind of traffic, all the vigor of nature that develops merely wastes itself without benefit to humanity, causing men to age prematurely.[43]

Infanticide is, similarly, the effect of an unavoidable dilemma in which a woman who has been seduced through weakness or overcome by violence finds herself forced to choose be-

43 [Cf. Montesquieu, Spirit, XII, 6: "The crime against nature will never make any great progress in society unless people are prompted to it by some particular custom, as among the Greeks, where the youths of that country performed all their exercises naked. . . . Let there be no customs preparatory to this crime; let it, like every other violation of morals, be severely proscribed by the civil magistrate; and nature will soon defend or resume her rights."]

tween infamy and the death of a being incapable of feeling
pains—how could she avoid preferring the latter to the inevitable misery awaiting her and her unfortunate infant? The
best way to prevent this crime would be through efficacious
laws protecting weakness against tyranny, which exaggerates
vices that cannot be concealed under a cloak of virtue.

I do not pretend to diminish the just horror which these
crimes merit, but having indicated their origins I believe I
can, with justice, derive a general conclusion—namely, that
one cannot call any punishment of a crime just in the precise
sense (that is to say, necessary) so long as the law has not made
use of the best means available, in the given circumstances of
a nation, to prevent it.

XXXVII

A PARTICULAR KIND OF CRIME

The reader of this work will notice that I have omitted a
class of crimes that has covered Europe with human blood
and has raised those awful piles where living human bodies
used to serve as food for flames, in the times when it was a
pleasing spectacle and agreeable harmony for the blind multitude to hear the muffled, confused groans of wretches that
issued out of the vortices of black smoke, the smoke of human
members, together with the crackling of charred bones and the
frying of still palpitating entrails. But reasonable men will see
that the place, the age, and the matter at hand do not permit
me to examine the nature of such a crime. It would take me
too long and too far away from my subject to prove how a
perfect uniformity of thought is necessary in a state, contrary
to the example of many nations; how opinions, distinguished
only by the subtlest and obscurest of differences, well beyond
the capacity of mortals, may nevertheless upset public order
when one of them is not authorized in preference to the others;
and how opinions are so constituted by nature that while some

of them, by contending and fermenting in opposition, gain in clarity, the true ones rising to the surface while the false sink into oblivion, others, uncertain and unsubstantial in themselves, need to be clothed with authority and force. It would take me too far to prove that, howsoever odious the imposition of force upon human minds may be, gaining for itself only dissimulation followed by debasement, and howsoever contrary it may seem to the spirit of gentleness and fraternity, commanded by reason and by the authority we most venerate, it is, nevertheless, necessary and indispensable. All of this should be taken as evidently proved and in conformity with the true interests of humanity, so long as it is actually practiced by someone with acknowledged authority. I speak only of the crimes that emanate from human nature and from the social contract, and not of sins, of which even the temporal punishments should be regulated according to principles other than those of a limited philosophy.[44]

XXXVIII

FALSE IDEAS OF UTILITY

One source of errors and injustices are the false ideas of utility formed by legislators.

False is the idea of utility that considers particular inconveniences before the general inconvenience, that commands feelings instead of exciting them, that says to logic: serve!

False is the idea of utility that sacrifices a thousand real advantages for one imaginary or trifling inconvenience; that would take fire from men because it burns, and water because one may drown in it; that has no remedy for evils, except destruction. The laws that forbid the carrying of arms are laws of such a nature. They disarm those only who are neither

[44] [Montesquieu is somewhat more explicit in his treatment of the crimes of witchcraft and heresy (*Spirit*, XII, 5). But Beccaria's appeal to authority here is probably ironic.]

inclined nor determined to commit crimes. Can it be supposed
that those who have the courage to violate the most sacred
laws of humanity, the most important of the code, will respect
the less important and arbitrary ones, which can be violated
with ease and impunity, and which, if strictly obeyed, would
put an end to personal liberty—so dear to men, so dear to the
enlightened legislator—and subject innocent persons to all the
vexations that the guilty alone ought to suffer? Such laws make
things worse for the assaulted and better for the assailants; they
serve rather to encourage than to prevent homicides, for an un-
armed man may be attacked with greater confidence than an
armed man. They ought to be designated as laws not preventive
but fearful of crimes, produced by the tumultuous impression of
a few isolated facts, and not by thoughtful consideration of the
inconveniences and advantages of a universal decree.

False is the idea of utility which would impose upon a multitude of sensible beings the symmetry and order to which
brutal and inanimate matter is subject, which ignores present
motives that are alone capable of exerting a constant and
powerful impression on a multitude in order to strengthen distant ones that make but a weak and transitory impression, unless magnified by a power of imagination rarely encountered
among men.

False, finally, is the idea of utility which, sacrificing the thing
to the name, distinguishes the public good from that of individuals. There is this difference between the state of society and
the state of nature, that the primitive man harms others no
more than is necessary to procure some advantage for himself;
the social man, on the contrary, is sometimes moved, by bad
laws, to injure others without advantage for himself. The despot casts fear and consternation into the heart of his slaves,
but it rebounds and returns with greater force to torment his
own heart. The more private and solitary fear is, the less dangerous is it to the person who makes it the instrument of his happiness; but the more it is public, and the greater the number of
people it affects, the more likely is it that some careless, or
desperate, or audaciously clever person will succeed in bend-

ing men to his purposes by inspiring them with pleasant expectations, made all the more appealing by the fact that the
risk of the enterprise is shared by a greater number; and, besides, the value the unhappy set upon their own existence
diminishes in proportion to their misery. This is the reason
why wrongs breed new wrongs; hate is a more lasting sentiment
than love—so much more lasting as the former acquires
strength from continuation of the acts that weaken the latter.

XXXIX

THE SPIRIT OF THE FAMILY

Baneful and authorized acts of injustice such as these have
been approved even by the most enlightened of men and practiced by the freest republics, as a consequence of having considered society to be an association of families rather than of
men. Suppose there are a hundred thousand men, or twenty
thousand families, each composed of five persons, including
the head who represents it: if it be an association consisting
of families, there will be twenty thousand men and eighty
thousand slaves; if of men, there will be a hundred thousand
citizens and not one slave. In the first case there will be a
republic, with twenty thousand little monarchies as its components; in the second, the republican spirit will breathe not
only in the public squares and in the popular assemblies but
also within the households, where men experience a large part
of their happiness or misery. Since laws and customs result
from the habitual sentiments of the members of a republic, in
the first case, where the members are heads of families, the
monarchic spirit will gradually make its way into the republic
itself, and its effect will be restrained only by the opposed
interests of individuals and not by any feeling that breathes of
liberty and equality. Family spirit is a spirit of details, limited
to trifling facts. The spirit that rules republics, sustained by
general principles, observes the facts and classifies them in the

order of their importance for the good of the majority. In the republic of families, children remain within the power of the head so long as he lives and are obliged to wait until his death for an existence dependent solely on the laws. Accustomed to submit and to fear in their youthful and most vigorous years, when the feelings are least affected by that timidity of experience which is called moderation, how shall they resist the obstacles that vice always opposes to virtue in the languid and declining years in which even the disposition to see what will come of them stands in the way of vigorous changes?

When the republic consists of men, orderly family relations are the result not of compulsion but of contract; and the children, when age liberates them from their natural dependence, which is that of weakness and the necessity of education and protection, become free members of the civil order, and they subject themselves to the head of the family in order to participate in its advantages, even as free men do in society at large. In the first instance, the children, that is, the largest and most useful part of the nation, are at the beck and call of their fathers; in the second, the sole binding tie is that sacred inviolable one we have of ministering necessary assistance to one another and of gratitude for benefits received, which is destroyed not so much by malice in the human heart as by an ill-conceived form of subjugation prescribed by the laws.

Such contradictions between the laws of a family and the fundamental principles of a commonwealth are a fertile source of other contradictions between domestic and public morality; they occasion, therefore, a perpetual conflict in every mind. Domestic morality inspires submission and fear; the other, courage and liberty: the first teaches the limitation of beneficence to a small number of persons, involving no spontaneous choice; the second calls for the extension of it to all classes of men. One commands a continual sacrifice of self to a vain idol, called "the good of the family" (which is often the good of no one of its components); the other teaches the pursuit of personal advantage without violation of the laws, or else it excites patriotic self-sacrifice with the reward of fanaticism which anticipates deeds. Such contrasts make men disdainful of pursuing virtue, which they find entangled and confused, and at that great distance from them in which all objects, physical as well as moral, appear to be when enveloped in obscurity. How often is a man, looking back on his past actions, astonished at finding himself dishonest!

The more society grows, the smaller part of the whole does each member become, and the republican sentiment diminishes proportionately if the laws neglect to reinforce it. Societies have, like human bodies, their circumscribed limits, increasing beyond which the economy is necessarily disturbed. It would seem that the size of a state ought to vary inversely with the sensibility of its constituency; otherwise, with both of them increasing, good laws would be obstructed in preventing crimes by the good they have themselves produced. A republic grown too vast can escape despotism only by subdividing and then reuniting itself as a number of federated little republics. But how is this to be realized? By a despotic dictator with the courage of Sulla [45] and as much genius for building up as he had for destroying. Such a man, if he be ambitious, has the glory of all the ages awaiting him; if he is a philosopher, the blessings of his fellow citizens will console him for the loss of authority, even supposing him not to have become indifferent to their gratitude. To the extent that our patriotic feelings weaken, our feelings for things immediately around us grow stronger; under the most extreme despotism, therefore, friendships are more lasting, and domestic virtues, always of a low order, are the most common, or, rather, the only ones. It should now be evident to everyone how very limited the views of most legislators have been.

45 [Lucius Cornelius Sulla (138-78 B.C.). Dictator of Rome from 82 to 79 B.C.]

XL

THE PUBLIC TREASURY

There was once a time when almost all penalties were pecuniary. The crimes of men were the prince's patrimony; attempts against the public security were an object of gain, he who was designated to defend it had an interest in seeing it offended. The object of punishments was, therefore, litigation between the treasury (exactor of these punishments) and the criminal—a civil affair, contentious, private rather than public, which assigned to the treasury other rights than those ordained for public protection, and to the criminal other wrongs than those to which he was subject for the sake of providing an example. The judge was, therefore, an advocate for the treasury rather than an impartial inquirer after truth, a revenue agent rather than the protector and minister of the laws. But as in this system confessing oneself delinquent meant confessing oneself a debtor to the treasury, which was the intent of criminal procedures at that time, so the confession of a crime, a confession so prepared as to favor and not to injure fiscal interests, became and still remains (the effects always outlasting the causes) the center around which all criminal procedures turn.

Without such a confession, a criminal convicted by indubitable proofs will incur a punishment lighter than the one officially decreed; without it he will not be subjected to torture for the sake of crimes of the same kind that he may have committed. But with a confession the judge takes possession of the criminal's person and torments him with methodical formalities in order to extract from him, as from an acquired land, the most profit he can. Having established the existence of a crime, the confession becomes a convincing proof; to make this proof less suspect, it is exacted forcibly through the agonies and desperation of pain, while, at the same time, an extra-judicial confession full of calm and indifference, unaffected by the overpowering fears of a trial by torture, is insufficient for condemnation. Inquiries and proofs that clarify the fact are set aside if they run counter to the interests of the treasury; it is not out of consideration for misery and weakness that a criminal is sometimes spared torments, but because of the possible losses this entity, now quite imaginary and inconceivable, might suffer. The judge becomes an enemy of the accused, of a chained man, prey to the horrors of squalor, torture, and a most terrible future; he does not look for the truth of the fact but for the crime in the prisoner; he lays snares for him and, if they fail, believes he has personally lost something and has undermined the sense of infallibility which man arrogates to himself in all things. The judge has the power to decide what inquiries suffice for imprisonment; in order that a person may prove himself innocent he must first be declared guilty. This is what is called an *offensive prosecution*—the typical form of criminal procedure in almost every part of enlightened Europe in the eighteenth century. The true prosecution, the *informative,* that is, the impartial inquiry into the fact, which reason commands, which the military laws use, which even Asiatic despotism allows in non-violent and unimportant cases, is rarely used in European tribunals. What a complicated labyrinth of strange absurdities which a happier posterity will, no doubt, find incredible! Only the philosophers of that time will be able to find, by searching in the nature of man, any verification that such a system was ever possible.

XLI

HOW TO PREVENT CRIMES

It is better to prevent crimes than to punish them. This is the ultimate end of every good legislation, which, to use the general terms for assessing the good and evils of life, is the art of leading men to the greatest possible happiness or to the least possible unhappiness.

But heretofore, the means employed have been false and contrary to the end proposed. It is impossible to reduce the turbulent activity of mankind to a geometric order, without any irregularity and confusion. As the constant and very simple laws of nature do not impede the planets from disturbing one another in their movements, so in the infinite and very contrary attractions of pleasure and pain, disturbances and disorder cannot be impeded by human laws. And yet this is the chimera of narrow-minded men when they have power in their grasp. To prohibit a multitude of indifferent acts is not to prevent crimes that might arise from them, but is rather to create new ones; it is to define by whim the ideas of virtue and vice which are preached to us as eternal and immutable. To what should we be reduced if everything were forbidden us that might induce us to crime! It would be necessary to deprive man of the use of his senses. For one motive that drives men to commit a real crime there are a thousand that drive them to commit those indifferent acts which are called crimes by bad laws; and if the probability of crimes is proportionate to the number of motives, to enlarge the sphere of crimes is to increase the probability of their being committed. The majority of the laws are nothing but privileges, that is, a tribute paid by all to the convenience of some few.

Do you want to prevent crimes? See to it that the laws are clear and simple and that the entire force of a nation is united in their defense, and that no part of it is employed to destroy them. See to it that the laws favor not so much classes of men as men themselves. See to it that men fear the laws and fear nothing else. For fear of the laws is salutary, but fatal and fertile for crimes is one man's fear of another. Enslaved men are more voluptuous, more depraved, more cruel than free men. These study the sciences, give thought to the interests of their country, contemplate grand objects and imitate them, while enslaved men, content with the present moment, seek in the excitement of debauchery a distraction from the emptiness of the condition in which they find themselves. Accustomed to an uncertainty of outcome in all things, the outcome of their crimes remains for them problematical, to the advantage of the passions that determine them. If uncertainty regarding the laws befalls a nation which is indolent because of climate, its indolence and stupidity are confirmed and increased; if it befalls a voluptuous but energetic nation, the result is a wasteful diffusion of energy into an infinite number of little cabals and intrigues that sow distrust in every heart, make treachery and dissimulation the foundation of prudence; if it befalls a brave and powerful nation, the uncertainty is removed finally, but only after having caused many oscillations from liberty to slavery and from slavery back to liberty.

Do you want to prevent crimes? See to it that enlightenment accompanies liberty. Knowledge breeds evils in inverse ratio to its diffusion, and benefits in direct ratio. A daring impostor, who is never a common man, is received with adorations by an ignorant people, and with hisses by an enlightened one. Knowledge, by facilitating comparisons and by multiplying points of view, brings on a mutual modification of conflicting feelings, especially when it appears that others hold the same views and face the same difficulties. In the face of enlightenment widely diffused throughout the nation, the calumnies of ignorance are silenced and authority trembles if it be not armed with reason. The vigorous force of the laws, meanwhile, remains immovable, for no enlightened person can fail to approve of the clear and useful public compacts of mutual security when he compares the inconsiderable portion of useless liberty he himself has sacrificed with the sum total of liberties sacrificed by other men, which, except for the laws, might have been turned against him. Any person of sensibility, glancing over a code of well-made laws and observing that he has lost only a baneful liberty to injure others, will feel constrained to bless the throne and its occupant.

It is not true that the sciences have always been injurious to mankind; when they were, the evil for men was inevitable. The multiplication of the human species on the face of the earth introduced war, the ruder arts, the first laws, which were temporary pacts arising out of necessity and dying with it.

This was the first philosophy of mankind, whose few components were just, because their indolence and little sagacity kept them from error. But the needs of men continued to multiply with the multiplication of their numbers. Stronger and more lasting impressions were necessary, therefore, to prevent frequent lapses into their primitive state of unsociability, which became more and more dangerous. Those primitive errors that populated the earth with false divinities and fashioned an invisible universe governing our own conferred a great good on mankind—I mean a great political good. Those who dared to take men by surprise, who dragged docile ignorance to the altars, were benefactors of men. By offering them things that lay beyond the reach of the senses, that fled before them the closer they believed themselves to be—things never despised because never well understood—those benefactors united and concentrated the divided passions of men upon a single object of much concern to them. These were the first experiences of all the nations that formed themselves out of primitive peoples; this was the epoch of formation for the great societies of men, and such was their necessary and perhaps only bond. I do not speak of that chosen people of God, for whom the most extraordinary miracles and the most signal favors served instead of human policy. But as error tends naturally to subdivide itself ad infinitum, so the sciences that arose out of it made of mankind a fanatical and blind multitude, shut up in a closed labyrinth, pushing and upsetting one another in such a way that some sensitive and philosophic spirits have regarded with envy even the ancient savage state. Such is the first epoch of man, in which knowledge or, let us say, rather, opinions are hurtful.

The second [epoch of mankind] lies in the difficult and terrible passage from errors to truth, from uncomprehended obscurity to light. The mighty clash of errors useful to a few powerful persons with truths useful to the many weak, the concentration and ferment of passions aroused at such a time, bring infinite harm upon miserable humanity. Whoever reflects upon the histories of nations which, after certain intervals of time resemble one another in their principal epochs, will often find that an entire generation has been sacrificed to the happiness of those that are to follow in the sad but necessary passage from the shadows of ignorance to the light of philosophy and from tyranny to liberty, which are its consequences. But, after spirits have been calmed and the flame which purged the nation of the ills that oppressed it has been extinguished, when truth, after progressing slowly at first and then rapidly, sits at last as a companion to monarchs on their thrones and enjoys a cult and altar in the parliaments of republics, who will ever dare to assert that enlightenment diffused among the multitude is more injurious than shadows, and that for men to understand correctly the true and simple relation of things is harmful to them?

If it be true that blind ignorance is less fatal than slight and confused knowledge, because this adds to the evils of the first those of error, which are unavoidable when one's vision falls short of the truth, then an enlightened man is the most precious gift the sovereign may bestow upon the nation and upon himself, making him the depository and guardian of the sacred laws. Used to seeing truth without fearing it, unaffected by most of the needs of reputation, which can never be sufficiently satisfied and which put the virtue of most men on trial; accustomed to contemplate humanity from the most elevated points of view, in his presence his own nation becomes a family of men joined as brothers, and the distance separating the mighty from the common people seems to him so much the less as the mass of humanity he has before his eyes is greater. Philosophers acquire needs and interests unknown to ordinary men, chief among which is that of not denying in public the principles they have taught in obscurity; they also acquire the habit of loving truth for its own sake. A selection of such men constitutes the happiness of a nation, but a merely temporary happiness, unless good laws so augment their number as to diminish the probability, which is always considerable, of a poor election.

Another way of preventing crimes is to direct the interest of the magistracy as a whole to observance rather than corruption of the laws. The greater the number of magistrates, the less dangerous is the abuse of legal power; venality is more difficult among men who observe one another, and their interest in increasing their personal authority diminishes as the portion that would fall to each is less, especially in comparison with the danger involved in the undertaking. If the sovereign, with his apparatus and pomp, with the severity of his edicts, with the permission he grants for unjust as well as just claims to be advanced by anyone who thinks himself oppressed, accustoms his subjects to fear magistrates more than the laws, [the magistrates] will profit more from this fear than personal and public security will gain from it.

Another way of preventing crimes is to reward virtue. Upon this subject I notice a general silence in the laws of all the nations of our day. If the prizes offered by the academies to discoverers of useful truths have increased our knowledge and have multiplied good books, why should not prizes distributed by the beneficent hand of the sovereign serve in a similar way to multiply virtuous actions? The coin of honor is always inexhaustible and fruitful in the hands of the wise distributor.

Finally, the surest but most difficult way to prevent crimes is by perfecting education—a subject much too vast and exceeding the limits I have prescribed for myself, a subject, I venture also to say, too intimately involved with the nature of government for it ever to be, even in the far-off happy ages of society, anything more than a barren field, only here and there cultivated by a few sages. A great man, who enlightens the world that persecutes him,[46] has indicated plainly and in detail what principal maxims of education are truly useful to men: they are, that it should consist less in a barren multiplicity of things than in a selection and precise definition of them; in substituting originals for the copies of the moral as well as physical phenomena which chance or willful activity may present to the fresh minds of youths; in leading them

[46] [Reference is to Rousseau's *Émile*.]

toward virtue by the easy way of feeling, and in directing them away from evil by the infallible one of necessity and inconvenience, instead of by the uncertain means of command which obtains only simulated and momentary obedience.

XLII

CONCLUSION

From what has thus far been demonstrated, one may deduce a general theorem of considerable utility, though hardly conformable with custom, the usual legislator of nations; it is this: *In order for punishment not to be, in every instance, an act of violence of one or of many against a private citizen, it must be essentially public, prompt, necessary, the least possible in the given circumstances, proportionate to the crimes, dictated by the laws.*[47] *Arent' like lots of judicial discretion*

[47] [See Article VIII of the "Declaration of the Rights of Man and of the Citizen," passed by the revolutionary National Assembly of France, on August 26, 1789: "The law ought to impose no other penalties but such as are absolutely and evidently necessary; and no one ought to be punished, but in virtue of a law promulgated before the offense, and legally applied."]